Easy Quattro Pro®

Shelley O'Hara

Easy Quattro Pro®

Copyright © 1991 by Que® Corporation.

Library of Congress Catalog No.: 91-62462

ISBN: 0-88022-798-2

93 92 91   6 5 4 3 2 1

Interpretation of the printing code: the rightmost double-digit number is the year of the book's printing; the rightmost single-digit number, the number of the book's printing. For example, a printing code of 91-1 shows that the first printing of the book occurred in 1991.

Screen reproductions in this book were created using Collage Plus from Inner Media, Inc., Hollis, NH.

Easy Quattro Pro is based on Quattro Pro Version 3.0.

Publisher: Lloyd J. Short

Associate Publisher: Karen A. Bluestein

Project Development Manager: Mary Bednarek

Managing Editor: Paul Boger

Book Design: Scott Cook, Karen A. Bluestein

Illustrations: Scott Cook

Production Team: Jill Bomaster, Sandy Grieshop, Bob LaRoche, Michele Laseau

Series Director
Karen A. Bluestein

Project Leader
Kathie-Jo Arnoff

Production Editor
Cindy Morrow

Editor
Patricia A. Brooks

Technical Editor
Robin Drake

Novice Reviewer
Linda E. Short

Quattro Pro is a registered trademark of Borland International, Inc.

Contents at a Glance

Easy Quattro Pro

Contents

Easy **Quattro Pro**

Contents

Easy **Quattro Pro**

Introduction

Quattro Pro is a spreadsheet program, which is an electronic accountant's pad. Rather than total figures using a pencil and column-ruled paper, you enter data into a Quattro Pro spreadsheet. You can then manipulate the data in that spreadsheet. With a spreadsheet program, you can perform simple mathematical operations—such as addition, subtraction, multiplication, and division—as well as calculate complex equations.

You can use Quattro Pro to keep track of facts (clients, for example) and figures (sales results, for example). You can create simple spreadsheets or complex financial models.

You can use Quattro Pro to create a variety of spreadsheets, including:

- Home Budget
- Business Budget
- Sales Report
- Business Expense Report
- Financial Report
- Check Register
- Inventory List
- Personnel List
- Client List
- Grade List

Budget

	Qtr 1	Qtr 2	Qtr 3	Qtr 4
Rent	10,000	10,000	10,000	10,000
Utilities	1,600	1,500	1,800	1,600
Supplies	320	320	320	320
Salaries	30,000	30,000	30,000	30,000
Taxes	1,500	500	500	500
Other	3,000	2,000	2,500	3,500
Total	$46,420	$44,320	$45,120	$45,920

Final Grades

Last Name	First Name	Midterm	Final	Average	Grade
Ackerman	Drew	75	77	76	C
Cady	Barb	96	88	92	A
Covent	Sarah	82	88	85	B
Diamond	Katie	94	90	92	A
Ford	Francis	98	98	98	A
Greene	Chris	90	84	87	B
Kincaid	Keenan	86	84	85	B
Lepperelli	Joe	75	73	74	C
Macy	Tyler	88	86	87	B
Miller	Tom	64	62	63	D
Moore	Antonia	96	98	97	A
Riley	Maggie	94	90	92	A
Silverman	Bart	60	66	63	D
Smith	Jodie	66	78	72	C
Smith	Xavier	87	83	85	B
Sullivan	Kelley	88	78	83 .	B
Wagner	Pam	80	82	81	B

While you can create all these documents without a spreadsheet program, Quattro Pro makes it easier to do so. For example, you can use Quattro Pro to

Calculate. You can write simple formulas to add, subtract, multiply, and divide. You tell Quattro Pro what numbers to use, and you can depend on Quattro Pro to calculate the results correctly every time.

Change data and recalculate. You can change, add, or delete data, and Quattro Pro recalculates the results automatically. You don't have to erase and rewrite when you forget a crucial figure.

Rearrange data. With your spreadsheet on-screen, you can add or delete a column or row. You can copy and move data from one place to another.

Repeat information. You can copy text, a value, or a formula to another place in the spreadsheet.

Reverse changes. Using the Undo feature, you can restore data that you just deleted, moved, or copied back to its original form.

Inventory

Stock #	Title	Category	Year
101	Total Recall	Action	1990
102	Godfather III	Drama	1990
103	Home Alone	Comedy	1990
104	Ghost	Romance	1990
105	Pretty Woman	Romance	1990
106	Good Fellas	Drama	1990
107	Dances with Wolves	Drama	1990
108	Freshman	Drama	1990
109	Kindergarten Cop	Action	1990
110	Presumed Innocent	Drama	1990

Financial Report for Central Library

Income		
	Fines and Fees	$447,965.87
	Taxes	$5,586,674.95
	State Funds	$86,868.11
	Federal Funds	$164,600.47
	Interest	$7,321,303.00
Total		$13,607,412.40
Expenses		
	Salaries	$9,040,130.52
	Books	$2,170,167.72
	Utilities	$528,997.33
	Services	$967,961.95
	Supplies	$279,961.95
Total		$12,987,219.47
Profit		$620,192.93

Change the format of data. You can format your results many different ways. For example, you can display a number with dollar signs, as a percentage, or as a date. You can align text left, right, or center.

Add enhancements. The heart of Quattro Pro is its calculation capabilities, but the results are what you use. In addition to controlling how data is displayed, you can call attention to results by adding shading, underlining data, drawing a box around data, and adding headers or footers.

Copy and reuse your spreadsheet. You can make a copy of a spreadsheet and make changes to create a second, different spreadsheet. For example, you can use the same format for a sales spreadsheet for each division of your company. Use the copy of the spreadsheet, enter the new data, and you have a new spreadsheet.

Business Expenses

DATE	EXPENSE	AMOUNT
01-Aug-91	Subscription	$160.00
05-Aug-91	Lunch	$35.00
09-Aug-91	Airfare	$560.00
09-Aug-91	Car Rental	$199.00
09-Aug-91	Hotel	$425.00
19-Aug-91	Class	$1,250.00
21-Aug-91	Lunch	$45.00
Total		$2,674.00

You can create thousands of spreadsheets in Quattro Pro. For example, you can use the program to keep track of stocks, investments, and inventory. You can create balance sheets and income statements. You can calculate personal or business expenses. You can keep lists of clients and employees. The examples in this introduction show just a couple of the spreadsheets that you can create using Quattro Pro.

Why You Need This Book

Quattro Pro's numerous features make working with numbers easy. Using this program, you can save time and make your work more efficient. But learning to use the many features is difficult at first, which is why you need this book.

This book is designed to make learning Quattro Pro *easy*. The book helps the beginning Quattro Pro user perform basic operations. Following the step-by-step instructions, you can learn to take advantage of Quattro Pro's functions and capabilities.

You don't need to worry that your knowledge of computers or Quattro Pro is too limited to use the program well. This book teaches you all that you need to know.

Reading this book will build your confidence. It will show you what steps are necessary to get a particular job done.

How This Book Is Organized

This book is designed with you, the beginner, in mind. It is divided into several parts:

- Introduction
- The Basics
- Task/Review
- Reference

The Introduction explains how the book is set up and how you can use it.

The next part, The Basics, outlines general information about your computer and its keyboard layout. This part explains basic concepts, such as moving around within your spreadsheets, selecting commands, and understanding the screen display.

The main part, Task/Review, tells you how to perform specific tasks. Each Task includes numbered steps that tell you the keys to press to complete a specific sample exercise. Before and After screens illustrate the exercise.

The last part, Reference, contains a glossary of common computer and Quattro Pro terms. This part also contains a quick reference of the most commonly used features of Quattro Pro, along with the keystrokes that are necessary to access these features.

How To Use This Book

This book is set up so that you can use it several different ways:

- You can read the book from start to finish.

- You can start reading at any point in the book.

- You can experiment with one exercise, many exercises, or all exercises.

- You can look up specific tasks that you want to accomplish, such as copying a cell.

- You can flip through the book, looking at the Before and After pictures, to find specific tasks.

- You can read only the exercise, only the review, or both the exercise and review sections. As you learn the program, you might want to follow along with the exercises. After you learn the program, you can refer to the Review to remind yourself how to perform a specific task.

- You can read any part of the exercises that you want. You can read all the text to see both the steps to follow and the explanation of the steps. You can read only the text in red to see the keystrokes to press. You can read only the explanation to understand what happens during a particular step.

Task section

The Task section includes numbered steps that tell you how to accomplish certain tasks, such as saving a spreadsheet or setting the column width. The numbered steps walk you through a specific example so that you can learn the task by doing it. Blue text below the numbered steps explains the concept in more detail.

Oops! notes

You may find that you performed a task that you do not want after all. The Oops! notes tell you how to undo each procedure or explain how to get out of a situation. By showing you how to reverse nearly every procedure or get out of nearly every mode, these notes allow you to use Quattro Pro more confidently.

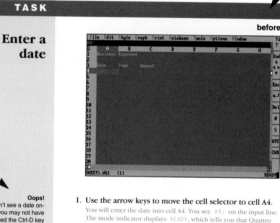

TASK

before

Enter a date

Oops!
If you don't see a date on-screen, you may not have pressed the Ctrl-D key combination before you typed the entry. Delete the entry and try again.

1. **Use the arrow keys to move the cell selector to cell A4.**
   You will enter the date into cell A4. You see A4: on the input line. The mode indicator displays READY, which tells you that Quattro Pro is ready to accept an entry.

2. **Press Ctrl-D.**
   The Ctrl-D key combination tells Quattro Pro that you want to enter a date. The mode indicator changes to DATE. If you type the date without pressing Ctrl-D, Quattro Pro tries to enter the date as a value. If you type 8-14-91, for example, Quattro Pro interprets the entry as 8 minus 14 minus 91. Quattro Pro evaluates the formula and displays the mathematical result, rather than the date, in the cell.

3. **Type 18-Jun.**
   18-Jun is one of Quattro Pro's acceptable date formats. To enter a date, you must use a format that Quattro Pro recognizes.

4. **Press Enter.**
   Pressing Enter enters the date. In the cell, you see 18-Jun; on the input line, you see a different number (33407). Quattro Pro stores dates as serial numbers. The numbering begins with 1 (December 31, 1899) and continues to the present date. Quattro Pro uses this format so that you can perform mathematical operations on dates (such as subtract two dates).

52

Easy Quattro

Before and After Illustrations

Each task includes Before and After illustrations that show how the computer screen will look before and after you follow the numbered steps in the Task section.

Review section

After you learn a procedure by following a specific example, you can refer to the Review section for a quick summary of the task. The Review section gives you the more generic steps for completing a task so that you can apply them to your own work. You can use these steps as a quick reference to refresh your memory about how to perform procedures.

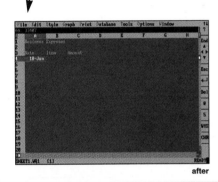

after

Delete an entry
To delete a date entry, press the Alt-F5 key combination immediately after entering the date.

REVIEW

1. Move the cell selector to the cell in which you want to enter the date.

2. Press the Ctrl-D key combination.

3. Type the date in one of these formats:

Format	Example
DD-MMM-YY	17-Mar-91
DD-MMM	17-Mar (assumes the current year)
MMM-YYYY	Mar 91 (assumes the first day of the month)
MM/DD/YY	03/17/91
MM/DD	03/17 (assumes the current year)

4. Press Enter.

To enter a date

Change column width
If you see asterisks in the column, the entry is too large to fit in the column. To change the column width, see *TASK: Set column width*.

Other notes

The sections may also contain short notes that tell you a little more about each procedure. These notes define terms, explain other options, and refer you to other sections, when applicable.

tering and Editing Data

53

How To Follow an Exercise

Quattro Pro is flexible because it enables you to perform a task many different ways. For consistency, this book makes certain assumptions about how your computer is set up and how you use Quattro Pro. As you follow along with each exercise, keep these key points in mind:

- This book assumes that you have a hard drive and that you followed the basic installation. This book assumes that you have installed a printer and that you have not changed any program defaults.

- This book assumes that you use the keyboard—that is, you access the menu by pressing the forward slash (/) key and typing the appropriate command letter. Remember that you can also access commands using the mouse.

- In the exercise sections, this book assumes that you are starting from the Before screen. If this screen contains any data, you should type the text shown in the screen.

- This book shows the screens in color. Your screens may appear in black and white or in different colors.

- Only the Before and After screens are illustrated. Screens are not shown for every step within an exercise.

- Each exercise is independent. That is, you don't have to complete any preceding exercises to follow along with the exercise that you want. If you do follow the exercises from start to finish, you have to create a new spreadsheet for each exercise. See *TASK: Create a new spreadsheet* for information on starting a new spreadsheet.

- As the tasks get more complex, the examples also are more complex. In some examples, the columns have been widened and the cells have been formatted.

Where To Get More Help

This book does not cover all Quattro Pro features or all ways of completing a task. This book is geared toward the beginning reader—a reader who wants just the basics. This reader isn't ready for advanced features such as using statistical functions or creating and formatting graphs. This book covers just the most common, basic features.

As you become more comfortable with Quattro Pro, you may need a more detailed reference book. Que Corporation offers several Quattro Pro books to suit your growing needs:

Using Quattro Pro 3, Special Edition

Quattro Pro 3 QuickStart

Quattro Pro 3 PC Tutor

Quattro Pro Quick Reference

Also of interest:

Que's Computer User's Dictionary, 2nd Edition

Introduction to Personal Computers

The Basics

Understanding Your Computer System

Using Your Keyboard

Understanding Key Terms

Understanding the Spreadsheet Screen

Entering Data

Making a Menu Selection

Selecting a Block

Saving and Retrieving Your Work

Easy Quattro Pro

Understanding Your Computer System

Your computer system is made up of these basic parts:

- The system unit
- The monitor
- The keyboard
- The floppy disk drive(s)
- The hard disk drive

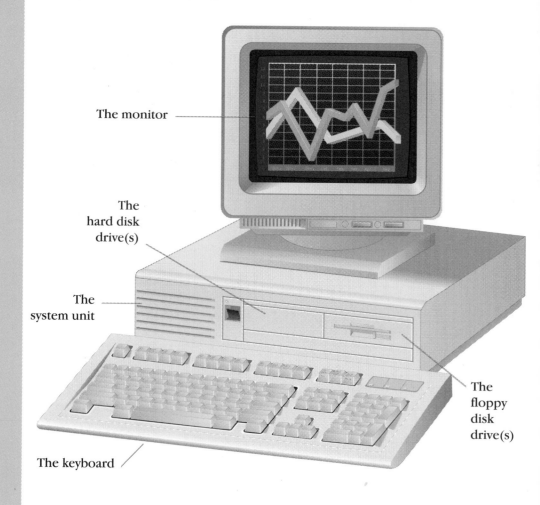

The monitor

The hard disk drive(s)

The system unit

The floppy disk drive(s)

The keyboard

You may also have a mouse and a printer.

14

System Unit.   This box holds all the electrical components of your computer. (The size of the system unit varies.) Somewhere on this box, you find an On/Off switch. (The location of the On/Off switch varies.) To use your computer, you must flip on the On/Off switch.

Monitor.   The monitor displays on-screen what you type on the keyboard. Your monitor may have a separate On/Off switch. Turn on this switch also.

Keyboard.   You use the keyboard to communicate with the computer. You use it to type entries and to issue commands. You type on the keyboard just as you do on a regular typewriter. A keyboard also has special keys. (Different computers have different keyboards.) These keys are discussed in the next section, *Using Your Keyboard*.

Floppy Disk Drive.   The floppy disk drive is the door into your computer. It enables you to put information into the computer and place it on the hard drive and to take information from the computer and place it on a floppy disk.

Hard Disk Drive.   A hard disk drive stores the programs and files with which you work. To use Quattro Pro, you must have a hard disk drive.

Printer.   The printer gives you a paper copy of your on-screen work. To print your spreadsheets, you need to attach and install a printer. Installing a printer tells Quattro Pro what printer you are using.

Mouse.   A mouse is a pointing device that enables you to move the cell selector on-screen and to perform other tasks. You don't need a mouse to use Quattro Pro.

Using Your Keyboard

A computer keyboard is just like a typewriter, only a keyboard has these additional keys:

- Function keys
- Arrow keys
- Other special keys

These keys are located in different places on different keyboards. For example, sometimes the function keys are located across the top of the keyboard. Sometimes they are located on the left side of the keyboard.

Your keyboard may also have a separate numeric keypad. You can use this keypad to move the cell selector or to enter numbers. See *Entering Numbers with the Numeric Keypad* later in this section.

For the following keyboard examples, this book uses the Enhanced keyboard. Your keyboard has the same keys, but they may be in a different location. You can familiarize yourself with the keyboard by reading the names on the keys.

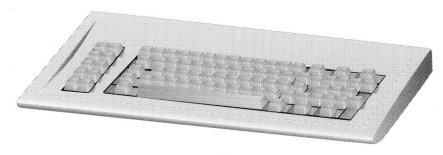

Original PC Keyboard

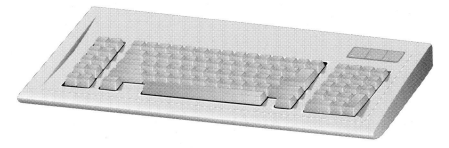

AT Keyboard

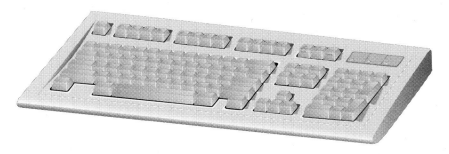

Enhanced Keyboard

Using the Forward Slash and Esc Keys

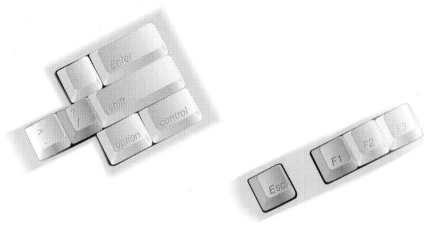

Two important keys to remember are the

- Forward slash (/) key
- Esc key

The forward slash (/) key activates the menu bar. After the menu bar is active, you can open a menu by typing the highlighted letter in that menu. Type /F, for example, to open the File menu. See *Making a Menu Selection* later in this section.

The Esc key is the "back out" key. It enables you to escape from most situations. For example, press the Esc key to cancel a menu command or to back out of a procedure.

Using the Function Keys

You can access some commands using function keys rather than using the menu. The Enhanced keyboard has 12 function keys labeled F1 through F12. You use the function keys to tell the computer to perform certain commands. You press the F1 key, for example, to display a help screen.

To access some features, you press another key with the function key. You press the Alt-F5 key combination, for example, to use Undo. In the text, a key combination is noted with a hyphen. Press and hold the first key, then press the second key.

Easy **Quattro Pro**

You will quickly memorize those function keys that you use frequently. To help you remember function keys, Quattro Pro provides a template that you place on your keyboard next to the function keys. This template reminds you of the use of function keys and function key combinations.

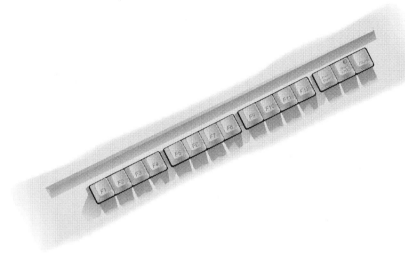

Using F1 (Help) and Alt-F5 (Undo)

Two important function keys (key combinations) are

- F1
- Alt-F5

F1 is the Help key. Press this key to get on-line help about a particular feature. See *TASK: Get help* for more information.

Alt-F5 is the Undo key combination. This key combination enables you to undo some changes. See *TASK: Use Undo* for more information.

Troubleshooting List

When you get into trouble, remember the keys and key combination just discussed (Esc, F1, and Alt-F5).

You can use these troubleshooting tips when in Quattro Pro:

- If you see a menu on-screen that you don't want open, press the Esc key until you return to the spreadsheet.

- If you see a prompt and you don't know how to respond correctly, press the Esc key until you return to the spreadsheet.

- If you see an error message, press the Esc key to clear the message.

- If you change your mind after performing an operation, press the Alt-F5 key combination.

- If you accidentally delete data, press the Alt-F5 key combination to restore the deleted text.

- If you want help on a particular topic, press the F1 key and then search the Help index for the topic that you want. See *TASK: Get help* for more information.

Moving the Cell Selector

You use the arrow keys to move the cell selector on-screen. Here is a list of the most common keys and key combinations:

To move	Press
To the first cell in the spreadsheet	Home
One cell right	→
One cell left	←
One row up	↑
One row down	↓
One screen left	Ctrl-← or Shift-Tab
One screen right	Ctrl-→ or Tab
One screen up	PgUp
One screen down	PgDn

Be careful! Don't press the Tab key to move to the next cell. Pressing the Tab key moves the cell selector one screen— rather than one cell—to the right. If you suddenly see a blank screen, you may have pressed the Tab key. Press Shift-Tab to move back one screen to the left.

Entering Numbers with the Numeric Keypad

You may have two sets of arrow keys: one used just to move the cell selector and one used to move the cell selector or to enter numbers. The second set is called the numeric keypad. These keys have both numbers and arrows on them.

To use the numeric keypad, press the Num Lock key. (Look for the words *Num Lock* or something similar on the key.) This key is a toggle; press the key to switch back and forth between numbers and arrows.

When you press the Num Lock key once, the keypad turns on the number lock and you can use the numbers. Press the key again to turn off the number lock and use the arrows on the keypad.

If you press an arrow key to move the cell pointer and numbers type on-screen instead, the Num Lock option is turned on. Press the Num Lock key again to turn it off.

Quattro Pro displays NUM in the status line when the Num Lock key is turned on.

Understanding Key Terms

To use Quattro Pro, you should understand the following key terms:

block.   A block can be a cell, a row, a column, or any rectangular area of columns and rows. After you select a block, you can perform different actions to it such as copy, erase, enhance, and so on. The Task/Review part of this book covers block operations.

block address.   The coordinates for a block of text. Quattro Pro identifies a block as follows: the first element in the block address is the location of the upper left cell in the block; the second element is the location of the lower right cell. The two elements are separated by two periods. For example, the block A1..C3 includes cells A1, A2, A3, B1, B2, B3, C1, C2, and C3.

cell.   The intersection of any column and row. Each cell in a spreadsheet has a unique address.

cell address.   The designation formed by combining the column and row locations into one description. For example, A8 describes the intersection of column A and row 8.

cell selector.   A highlighted rectangle that indicates the active cell. The cell selector shows where data is entered or a block begins.

directory.   A disk area that stores files. A directory is like a drawer in a file cabinet. Within that drawer, you can store several files.

file.   The various individual reports, spreadsheets, databases, and documents that you store on your hard drive (or disk) for future use.

formula.   An entry that performs a calculation using
   numbers, other formulas, or text.

function.   A built-in formula that is supplied with Quattro
   Pro. Functions perform specialized calculations for you,
   such as loan payments.

label.   A text entry.

spreadsheet.   The blank area of columns and rows that
   appears when you first start Quattro Pro. Also, all
   the data and formatting information that you enter
   on-screen. Quattro Pro keeps track of spreadsheets by
   storing them in files on disk.

value.   A number, formula, date, or time entry.

Understanding the Spreadsheet Screen

After you start the program, you see a blank spreadsheet
on-screen. First, take a look at the spreadsheet area; then
note some other important screen areas. If you want to start
the program and follow along, see *TASK: Start Quattro Pro*.
This task is the first one in the Task/Review part.

The Spreadsheet Area

The main part of the spreadsheet screen is the spreadsheet
area. A spreadsheet is a grid of columns and rows. A Quattro
Pro spreadsheet has 256 columns and 8,192 rows.

Columns are read from top to bottom and are numbered
with letters (A-Z, AB-AZ, and so on through IV).

Rows are read across the spreadsheet and are numbered
1 through 8192.

cell —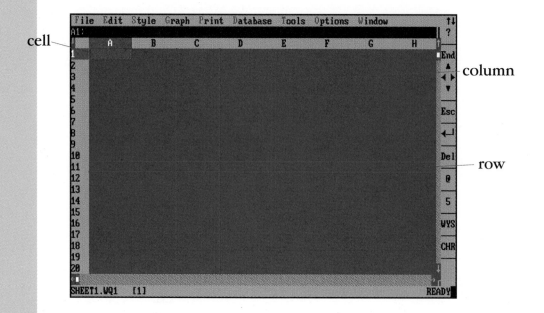— column

— row

A cell is the intersection of a column and row. The cell selector, which is a highlighted bar, indicates the active cell. Use the arrow keys to move the cell selector to a different cell.

Other Spreadsheet Areas

menu bar —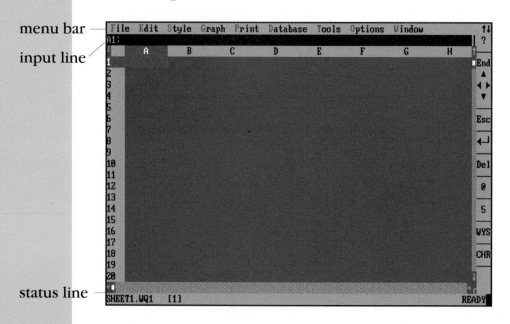
input line —

status line —

Other important spreadsheet areas are the

- menu bar
- input line
- status line

The menu bar is the first line on-screen. This line displays the main menu names (File, Edit, Style, Graph, Print, Database, Tools, Options, and Window). You access commands through the menu bar. To activate the menu bar, press the forward slash (/) key. See the section *Making a Menu Selection*.

The input line is the second line on-screen. This line displays information about the current cell. You see the cell address in this line. If you have entered something in the cell, you also see this entry on the input line. If you have formatted the line (added special enhancements such as italics or underlining), you see codes indicating the format change.

The status line is the last line on-screen. This line displays information about the active spreadsheet (file name), window (if you have more than one open), and modes (such as READY).

Notice that icons appear along the far right side of the screen. You can use these icons with the mouse. See *Using Quattro Pro 3,* Special Edition, for more information.

Entering Data

Quattro Pro accepts two types of data as valid entries: labels and values. A label is a text entry. A value can be a number, formula, date, or time.

The first character that you type tells Quattro Pro how to interpret the entry. If you type a number, Quattro Pro expects a value. If you type an alphabetic character (A–Z), Quattro Pro expects a label.

Entering a Label

To enter a label (text), position the cell selector in the cell that you want, type the entry, and press Enter. Quattro Pro precedes labels with a prefix. The prefix tells Quattro Pro that the entry is text, and it indicates how the entry should be aligned. The default alignment is left, which is indicated by an apostrophe.

Use labels as row and column headings and for all text entries, such as names, titles, and so on. You should also enter certain numbers (such as phone numbers, addresses, and social security numbers) as a label. These entries are text, as opposed to values that you would use in a formula.

To enter a number as a label (for example, a phone number), you must type an apostrophe first and then type the entry. If you type only the number, Quattro Pro interprets the entry as a value. If you type *555-3756*, for example, Quattro Pro interprets the entry as 555 *minus* 3756. Quattro Pro evaluates this formula and displays the result (in this example, –3201) in the cell instead of the number.

See *TASK: Enter text* for more information.

Entering a Number

To enter a number, position the cell selector in the cell that you want, type the value, and press Enter. To type a negative number, type a minus sign before the number. See *TASK: Enter a number* for more information.

Entering Other Values

You use special methods to enter dates, times, and formulas. These entries are also considered values.

See *TASK: Enter a date* and *TASK: Enter a time* for information on dates and times.

To enter a formula, refer to the following sections: *TASK: Add cells; TASK: Subtract cells; TASK: Multiply cells; TASK: Divide two cells; TASK: Total cells with the @SUM function;* and *TASK: Calculate an average*.

Editing Data

As you edit, you use three important editing keys:

- The Enter key
- The Del (or Delete) key
- The F2 key

To enter data in a cell, move the cell selector to that cell, type the entry, and press Enter. Pressing Enter confirms the entry and moves the data from the input line to the cell. You can also press the arrow keys to enter the data. See the tasks on entering text, numbers, dates, and so on for more information on entering data.

The Del key clears an entry. To clear a cell, move the cell selector to that cell and press the Del key. See *TASK: Erase a cell*.

To edit a cell, move the cell selector to that cell, press the F2 key, and then use the arrow keys to move to the characters that you want to change. Make the changes and then press Enter. See *TASK: Edit a cell*.

Making a Menu Selection

You access commands through Quattro Pro's menu system. Start by pressing the forward slash (/) key to activate the menu bar. When you press the forward slash key, a highlight bar appears in the menu bar. The File menu is highlighted.

Next, press the highlighted letter in the menu name. Type F, for example, to open the File menu. You can also use the arrow keys to move the highlight bar to the menu that you want to open and then press Enter.

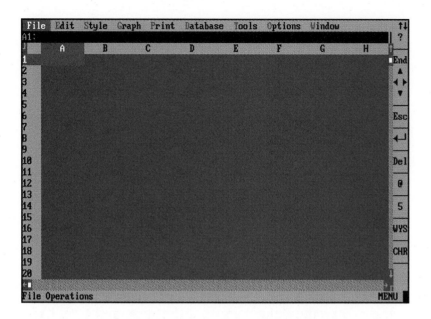

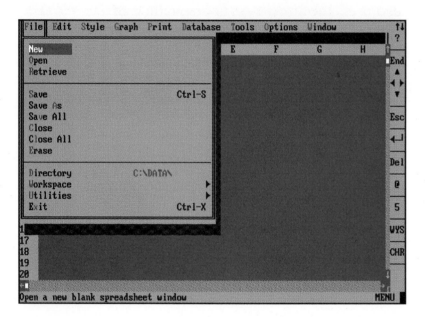

To select an option, type the highlighted letter in the option name. Type S, for example, to select Save. You can also use the arrow keys to move the highlight bar to the option and then press Enter.

Sometimes a second menu appears. Use the same procedure to access commands from a second menu.

Easy Quattro Pro

This book combines typing the forward slash (/) key with the highlighted letter. For example, some steps say "Type /FS." This notation means press the forward slash key to activate the menu bar, type F to select File, and then type S to select Save.

You can also use the mouse to select menu commands. Click on the menu name to open the menu; then click on the option that you want.

Sometimes you may display a menu that you don't want. To leave a menu without making a selection, press the Esc key.

Selecting a Block

A block is any rectangular section of the spreadsheet; it can be a cell, a column, a row, or a combination of contiguous columns and rows. You can perform many actions on a block, such as copy, move, format, and so on. These tasks are covered in the Task/Review part of the book.

One of the most important tasks to learn is selecting a block. Many of the exercises in this book assume that you preselect a block and then issue the command. You can also do the reverse—issue the command and then select the block.

There are many ways to select a block:

- Point to the block
- Use the mouse
- Type the block coordinates

Pointing to the Block

To preselect a block, press the Shift-F7 key combination to enter EXT mode, use the arrow keys to highlight the block that you want, and then issue the command.

If you issue the command first, you are prompted for the block. In this case, press the Shift-F7 key combination (or press the period key) to anchor the first cell and to enter POINT mode. Then use the arrow keys to highlight the block that you want. Press Enter to accept the block.

Selecting a Block with the Mouse

To preselect a block with the mouse, move the mouse pointer to the first cell that you want to include, press and hold the mouse button, and drag the mouse diagonally across the cells that you want to select. Release the mouse button. After you select the block, you can issue the command.

If you issue the command first, you can still use the mouse to point to the block. Use the same procedure: click on the first cell, press and hold the mouse button, and drag the mouse diagonally across the other cells.

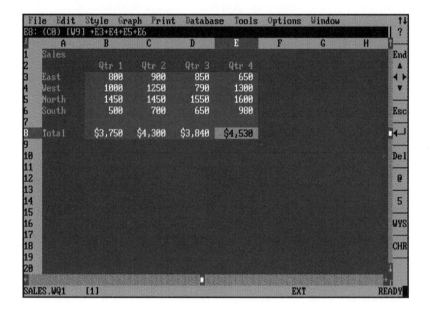

Typing the Block Address

If you select the command first, you are prompted to enter the block. In this case, you can type the block address. The block address consists of the upper left cell, two periods, and the lower right cell.

Easy **Quattro Pro**

Saving and Retrieving Your Work

All your work is stored temporarily in the computer's memory, which is like having a shopping list in your head. Until you commit the list to paper, you may forget some or all of the items. The same is true with Quattro Pro. Until you save the spreadsheet, you can lose all or part of your work.

Saving the spreadsheet doesn't commit it to paper like the shopping list. Saving the spreadsheet saves the data to your disk. Then when you need the spreadsheet again, you can retrieve it from the disk.

Quattro Pro does not automatically save your work. You should save every 5 or 10 minutes.

You have these choices when you want to save a document:

When you want to	Refer to
Save a spreadsheet that you have not saved	TASK: Save a spreadsheet for the first time
Open a spreadsheet that you have saved	TASK: Open a spreadsheet
Save a spreadsheet that you have saved once already	TASK: Save a spreadsheet again
Save a spreadsheet with a new name and keep the original	TASK: Save a spreadsheet with a new name
Start a new spreadsheet	TASK: Create a new spreadsheet
Clear the screen and abandon the spreadsheet on-screen; return to the previous version (if you have saved) or lose the current version (if you haven't saved)	TASK: Abandon the spreadsheet
Clear the screen, but save the spreadsheet	TASK: Close a spreadsheet

Task/Review

Entering and Editing Data

Managing Files

Formatting the Spreadsheet

Advanced Editing

Printing and Enhancing the Spreadsheet

Easy Quattro Pro

Alphabetical Listing of Tasks

Entering and Editing Data

This section covers the following tasks:

Start Quattro Pro

Exit Quattro Pro

Get help

Change to character display mode

Turn on Undo

Enter text

Enter a number

Enter a date

Enter a time

Add cells

Subtract cells

Multiply cells

Divide two cells

Overwrite a cell

Edit a cell

Erase a cell

Copy a cell

Move a cell

Go to a specific cell

Use Undo

Start Quattro Pro

before

C:\>

Oops!
If the program doesn't start, be sure that you typed the correct directory for the program files in step 4.

1. **Turn on the computer and monitor.**

   Every computer has a different location for its On/Off switch. Check the side, the front, and the back of your computer. Your monitor also may have a separate On/Off switch. If so, you also need to turn on the monitor.

2. **If necessary, respond to the prompts for date and time.**

   When you first turn on the computer, some systems ask you to enter the current time and date. (Many of the newer models enter the time and date automatically. If you aren't prompted for these entries, don't worry.)

   If the computer prompts you, type the current date and press Enter. Then type the current time and press Enter. The computer then adds the correct date and time to any files that you save. You should complete this step so that your file information is complete.

3. **Install the program.**

   To use Quattro Pro, the program must be installed. You need to install the program only once. (Follow the installation procedures outlined in the Quattro Pro manual that came with the software.) *Easy Quattro Pro* assumes that you have installed Quattro Pro on a hard drive in the \QPRO directory.

4. **Type cd\qpro.**

   QPRO is the name of the directory that stores the program files. If you have stored your program in a different directory, type that name instead of QPRO.

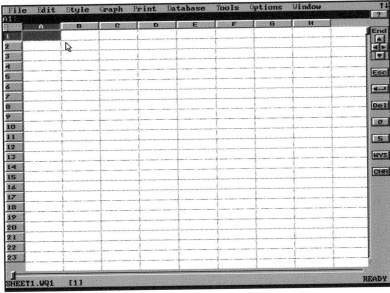

after

5. **Press Enter.**

   Pressing Enter places you in the Quattro Pro directory. You see the prompt `C:\QPRO>`.

6. **Type q.**

   Typing q starts the program.

7. **Press Enter.**

   Pressing Enter confirms the command and starts the Quattro Pro program. You see the opening screen for a few seconds; then you see a blank spreadsheet.

   The After screen shows Quattro Pro in WYSIWYG mode. You may see the screen in character mode. See *TASK: Change to character display mode.*

R E V I E W

To start Quattro Pro

1. Turn on your computer and monitor.

2. Respond to the prompts for the date and time, if necessary.

3. Make sure that the program has been installed.

4. Type **cd\qpro** and press **Enter.**

5. Type **q** and press **Enter.**

Exit Quattro Pro

```
File   Edit   Style   Graph   Print   Database   Tools   Options   Window   ↑↓
C10:  @SUM(C4..C8)                                                          ?
       A      B      C      D      E      F      G      H      I      J
 1                         Budget                                        End
 2                                                                        ⬚
 3            Jan    Feb                                                  ◄▷
 4    House   712    712                                                  Esc
 5    Utilities 180   190                                                 ⬚
 6    Car     270    325                                                  ↵
 7    Food    250    300                                                  Del
 8    Misc.   350    345                                                  ⬚
 9                                                                         G
10    Total   1762   1872                                                  S
11                                                                        WYS
12                                                                        CHR
13
14
15
16
17
18
19
20
21
22
23
SHEET1.WQ1   [1]                                              READY
```

Oops!
If you did not want to exit, type Q at the C:\QPRO> prompt to restart the program. See *TASK: Start Quattro Pro*.

1. **Save the spreadsheet.**

   See any of the tasks that discuss saving the spreadsheet in the next section.

2. **Type /FX.**

   Typing /FX selects the File Exit command. If you have saved the spreadsheet, you return to DOS.

C:\QPRO>

after

Try a shortcut
Press the Ctrl-X key combination to select the File Exit command.

1. Save the spreadsheet.

2. Type **/FX** to select the File Exit command.

To exit Quattro Pro

Did you save the spreadsheet?
If you have not saved the spreadsheet, Quattro Pro prompts you. Type N to return to the spreadsheet, Y to abandon any unsaved work, or S to save the spreadsheet and exit the program.

Get help

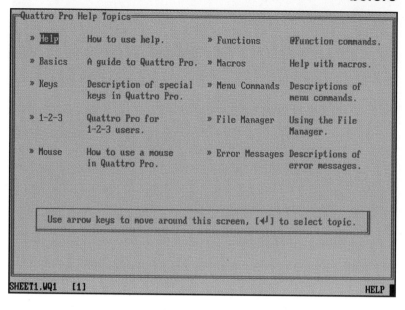

before

```
┌Quattro Pro Help Topics──────────────────────────────┐
│  » Help      How to use help.      » Functions    @Function commands.│
│                                                      │
│  » Basics    A guide to Quattro Pro.  » Macros    Help with macros.│
│                                                      │
│  » Keys      Description of special  » Menu Commands  Descriptions of│
│              keys in Quattro Pro.                  menu commands.│
│                                                      │
│  » 1-2-3     Quattro Pro for        » File Manager  Using the File│
│              1-2-3 users.                          Manager.│
│                                                      │
│  » Mouse     How to use a mouse     » Error Messages  Descriptions of│
│              in Quattro Pro.                       error messages.│
│                                                      │
│    ┌──────────────────────────────────────────────┐ │
│    │ Use arrow keys to move around this screen, [↵] to select topic.│ │
│    └──────────────────────────────────────────────┘ │
│                                                      │
└──────────────────────────────────────────────────────┘
SHEET1.WQ1   [1]                                    HELP
```

Oops!
To exit help, press the
Esc key.

1. **Press F1.**

   The F1 key is the Help key. You see a list of Quattro Pro help topics on-screen.

2. **Press the ↓ key four times.**

   Pressing the ↓ key moves the cell selector through the topics left to right. Pressing the ↓ key four times highlights the Keys topic. Select this topic to display help on special keys used in Quattro Pro.

3. **Press Enter.**

   Pressing Enter displays a list of help topics that discuss using the keyboard. The Function Keys topic is highlighted.

4. **Press Enter.**

   Pressing Enter selects the Function Keys topic. You see a list of function keys and their uses.

5. **Press Esc.**

   Pressing the Esc key exits help. You return to the spreadsheet.

Easy **Quattro Pro**

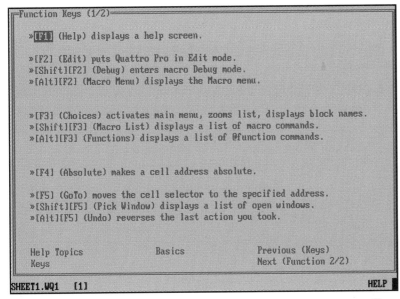

```
┌─Function Keys (1/2)══════════════════════════════════════╗
│                                                          │
│  »[F1] (Help) displays a help screen.                    │
│                                                          │
│  »[F2] (Edit) puts Quattro Pro in Edit mode.             │
│  »[Shift][F2] (Debug) enters macro Debug mode.           │
│  »[Alt][F2] (Macro Menu) displays the Macro menu.        │
│                                                          │
│                                                          │
│  »[F3] (Choices) activates main menu, zooms list, displays block names. │
│  »[Shift][F3] (Macro List) displays a list of macro commands. │
│  »[Alt][F3] (Functions) displays a list of @function commands. │
│                                                          │
│                                                          │
│  »[F4] (Absolute) makes a cell address absolute.         │
│                                                          │
│  »[F5] (GoTo) moves the cell selector to the specified address. │
│  »[Shift][F5] (Pick Window) displays a list of open windows. │
│  »[Alt][F5] (Undo) reverses the last action you took.    │
│                                                          │
│                                                          │
│  Help Topics            Basics           Previous (Keys)  │
│  Keys                                     Next (Function 2/2) │
│                                                          │
├──────────────────────────────────────────────────────────┤
│ SHEET1.WQ1   [1]                                    HELP ▐│
└──────────────────────────────────────────────────────────┘
```

after

1. Press F1 (Help).

2. Highlight the main topic that you want.

3. Press Enter.

4. Highlight the specific topic that you want.

5. Press Enter.

6. Press Esc to exit Help.

To get help

Change to character display mode

before

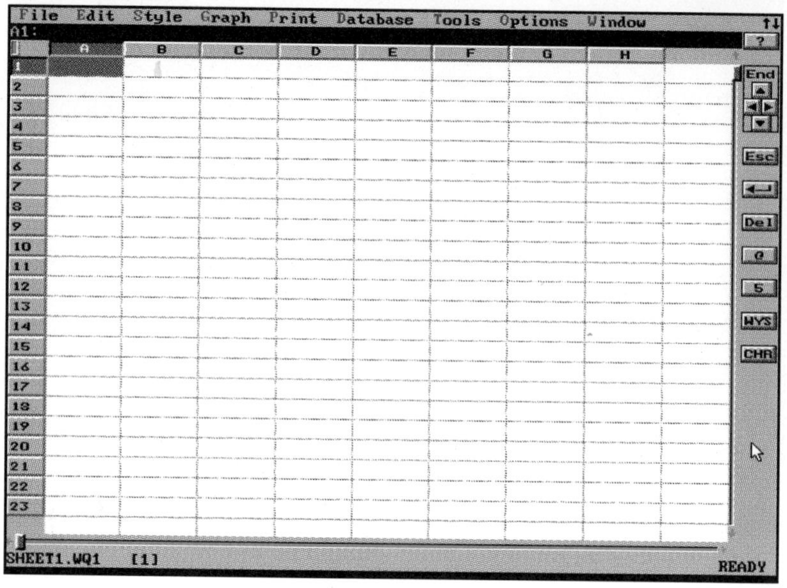

```
 File  Edit  Style  Graph  Print  Database  Tools  Options  Window    ↑↓
A1:                                                                      ?
       A      B      C      D      E      F      G      H
 1                                                                     End
 2                                                                      ◄►▲
 3                                                                       ▼
 4
 5                                                                     Esc
 6
 7                                                                      ◄┘
 8
 9                                                                     Del
10
11                                                                      ⊙
12
13                                                                      S
14
15                                                                     WYS
16
17                                                                     CHR
18
19
20
21                                                                      �k
22
23
SHEET1.WQ1    [1]                                                    READY
```

Oops!
If you don't see a change, you may already be using character mode. To return to WYSIWYG mode, see *TASK: Change to WYSIWYG mode.*

1. Type /OD.

Typing /OD selects the Option Display Mode command. You see a list of available display modes. Your list may be different, depending on your monitor.

The default display mode for Quattro Pro is WYSIWYG. WYSIWYG stands for What You See Is What You Get. This mode displays the spreadsheet as it will appear when printed.

When you are entering straight data, you will want to work in character mode. Switch to WYSIWYG mode when you are formatting the spreadsheet.

2. Type A.

Typing A selects the character display mode. The spreadsheet appears in character mode.

3. Type U.

Typing U selects the Update command. Now when you start Quattro Pro, you always see the character mode display.

The next time you start Quattro Pro, if you see the spreadsheet in WYSIWYG mode, you probably forgot this step. Be sure to tell Quattro Pro to update the settings.

Easy **Quattro Pro**

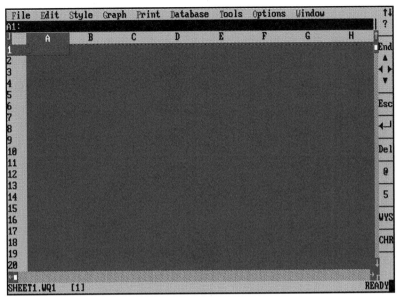

after

4. Type **Q**.

Typing Q selects the Quit command. You see the spreadsheet on-screen.

1. Type **/OD** to select the Options Display Mode command.

2. Type **A** to select character mode.

3. Type **U** to select the Update command and make character mode the default setting.

4. Type **Q** to close the menu.

To change to character display mode

What is character mode?
Character mode lets you see only text and minimal formatting on-screen. Most screens in this book show spreadsheets in character mode.

What is WYSIWYG mode?
WYSIWYG mode lets you see—on-screen—how a printed spreadsheet will look, with all its formatting and enhancements.

Turn on Undo

before

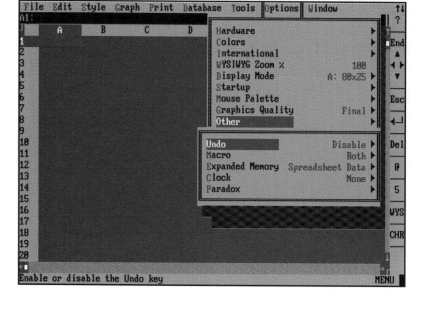

Oops!
If you try to use Undo and you receive an error message, you may not have typed U to update the settings. Follow this procedure again.

1. **Type /OO.**

   Typing /OO selects the Options Other command. You see a list of options that you can specify.

2. **Type U.**

   Typing U selects Undo. You see two choices: Enable and Disable.

3. **Type E.**

   Typing E selects Enable. Enable turns on the Undo feature for this work session.

4. **Type U.**

   Typing U updates the settings and saves them for future work sessions. Undo is now turned on whenever you start the program.

5. **Type Q.**

   Typing Q closes the menu.

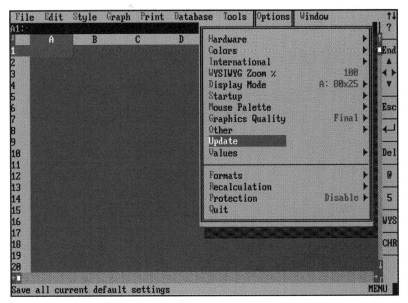

after

1. Type **/OO** to select the Options Other command.

2. Type **UE** to select Undo Enable.

3. Type **U** to select Update.

4. Type **Q** to close the menu.

To turn on Undo

Use Undo
To use the Undo feature, see *TASK: Use Undo*.

Enter text

before

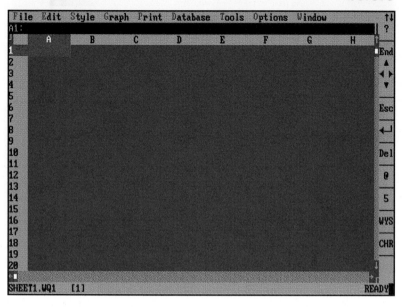

1. Press the → key **three times**.

When you open a blank spreadsheet, the cell selector is in cell A1. Pressing the → key three times moves the cell selector to cell D1. The active cell on a spreadsheet appears as a highlighted rectangle. This is the cell selector.

Each cell in a spreadsheet has a unique address. A cell address is formed by combining the column and row locations into one description. For example, D1 describes the intersection of column D and row 1.

You see D1: on the input line. The mode indicator displays READY, which tells you that Quattro Pro is ready to accept an entry.

2. Type **Budget**.

Budget is the title of your spreadsheet. The mode indicator changes to LABEL, which means that you are entering a label (text).

If you make a mistake, use the Backspace key to correct the entry. The entry is not entered into the cell until you press Enter or an arrow key.

3. Press **Enter**.

Pressing Enter accepts the entry on the input line and enters it into the cell. The cell selector remains in cell D1. You see the title on the input line preceded by an apostrophe. An apostrophe tells Quattro Pro that this entry is a label (text as opposed to a number or a formula). Your row and column headings also may be labels.

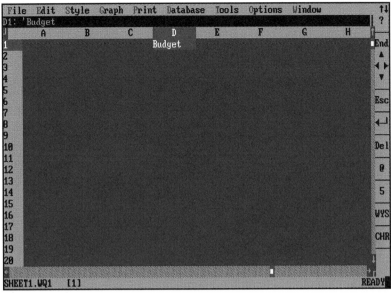

after

Notice that the entry is left-aligned, which is the default format for labels. To change this format, see the tasks on formatting the spreadsheet later in this book.

You can also press any of the arrow keys to accept the entry and move the cell selector.

To enter a number as a label (for example, a phone number), you must type an apostrophe first and then type the entry. If you type only the number, Quattro Pro interprets the entry as a value. If you type *555-3756*, for example, Quattro Pro interprets the entry as 555 *minus* 3756. The result of this equation (–3201), rather than the phone number, is displayed in the cell.

Delete a text entry
Delete a text entry by positioning the cell selector in the cell you want to erase and pressing the Del key.

R E V I E W

1. Move the cell selector to the cell in which you want to enter text.

2. Type the text.

3. Press **Enter** or any arrow key.

To enter text

Use the mouse
If you have a mouse, you can select a cell by pointing to the cell that you want and clicking the mouse button.

Enter a number

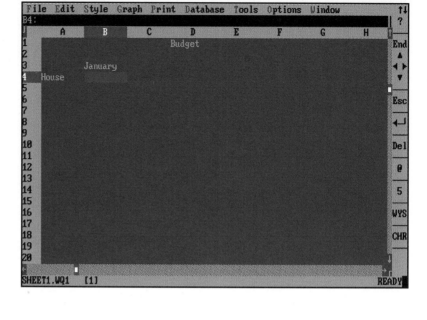

before

1. **Use the arrow keys to move to cell B4.**

   You will enter a number into cell B4. You see `B4:` on the input line. The mode indicator displays `READY`, which tells you that Quattro Pro is ready to accept an entry.

2. **Type 712.**

   712 is the number that you are entering into the cell. You see the value (712) displayed on the input line. The mode indictor changes to `VALUE`, which indicates that this entry is a value. A value can be a number, formula, date, or time.

   If you make a mistake, press the Esc key to delete the entry. The value is not entered into the cell until you press Enter or an arrow key.

Easy **Quattro Pro**

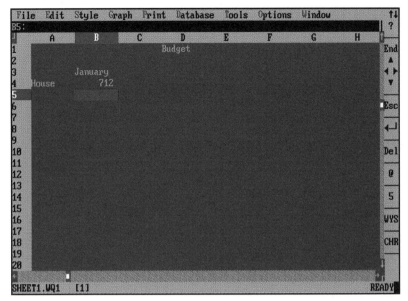

after

Delete a value
You can delete a value by placing the cell selector in the cell that you want to erase and pressing the Del key.

3. **Press the ↓ key once.**

Pressing the ↓ key once accepts the entry, enters the value into the cell, and moves the cell selector to the next row (cell B5).

Notice that the entry is right-aligned and that no decimal places, commas, or dollar signs are displayed. This is the default format for numbers. To change this format, see the tasks in the formatting section of this book.

REVIEW

To enter a number

1. Move the cell selector to the cell in which you want to enter the number.

2. Type the number.

3. Press **Enter** or any arrow key.

Enter a negative number
To enter a negative value, type a – (minus sign) and then type the value.

Enter a date

before

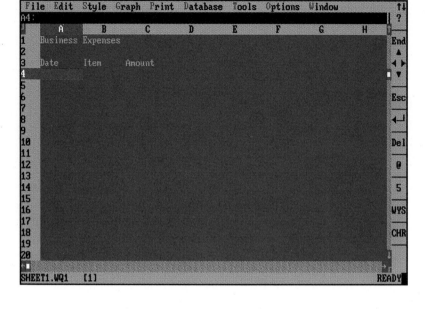

Oops!
If you don't see a date on-screen, you may not have pressed the Ctrl-D key combination before you typed the entry. Delete the entry and try again.

1. **Use the arrow keys to move the cell selector to cell A4.**

   You will enter the date into cell A4. You see A4: on the input line. The mode indicator displays READY, which tells you that Quattro Pro is ready to accept an entry.

2. **Press Ctrl-D.**

   The Ctrl-D key combination tells Quattro Pro that you want to enter a date. The mode indicator changes to DATE. If you type the date without pressing Ctrl-D, Quattro Pro tries to enter the date as a value. If you type *8-14-91*, for example, Quattro Pro interprets the entry as 8 *minus* 14 *minus* 91. Quattro Pro evaluates the formula and displays the mathematical result, rather than the date, in the cell.

3. **Type 18-Jun.**

   18-Jun is one of Quattro Pro's acceptable date formats. To enter a date, you must use a format that Quattro Pro recognizes.

4. **Press Enter.**

   Pressing Enter enters the date. In the cell, you see 18-Jun; on the input line, you see a different number (33407). Quattro Pro stores dates as serial numbers. The numbering begins with 1 (December 31, 1899) and continues to the present date. Quattro Pro uses this format so that you can perform mathematical operations on dates (such as subtract two dates).

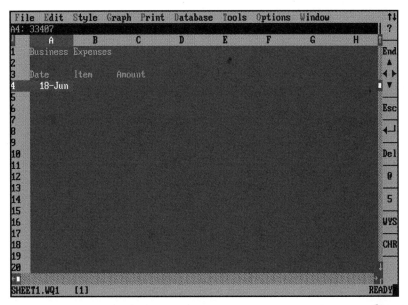

after

1. Move the cell selector to the cell in which you want to enter the date.

2. Press the **Ctrl-D** key combination.

3. Type the date in one of these formats:

Format	*Example*
DD-MMM-YY	17-Mar-91
DD-MMM	17-Mar (assumes the current year)
MMM-YYY	Mar 91 (assumes the first day of the month)
MM/DD/YY	03/17/91
MM/DD	03/17 (assumes the current year)

4. Press **Enter**.

To enter a date

Change column width
If you see asterisks in the column, the entry is too large to fit in the column. To change the column width, see *TASK: Set column width*.

Entering and Editing Data

53

Enter a time

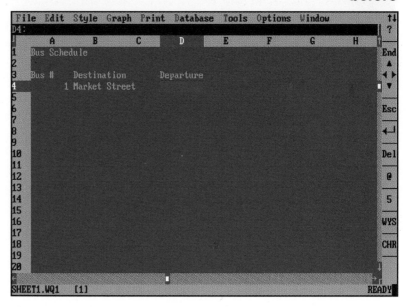

Oops!
If you don't see a time on-screen, you may not have pressed the Ctrl-D key combination before you typed the entry. Delete the entry and try again.

1. **Use the arrow keys to move the cell selector to cell D4.**

    You see D4: on the input line. The mode indicator displays READY, which tells you that Quattro Pro is ready to accept an entry.

2. **Press Ctrl-D.**

    Pressing the Ctrl-D key combination tells Quattro Pro that you want to enter a time. The mode indicator displays DATE. If you type the time without pressing the Ctrl-D key combination, Quattro Pro tries to enter the time as a number. You either receive an error message or type an incorrect entry.

3. **Type 10:00.**

    10:00 is one of Quattro Pro's acceptable time formats. To enter a time, you must use a format that Quattro Pro recognizes.

4. **Press Enter.**

    In the cell, you see 10:00; on the input line, you see a different number (0.41666666666667). Quattro Pro stores times as serial numbers. Quattro Pro uses this format so that you can perform mathematical operations on times (such as subtracting two times).

Easy **Quattro Pro**

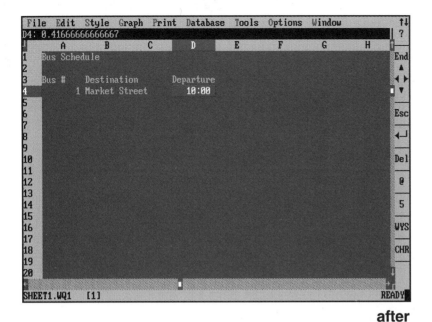

after

Delete an entry
To delete the time, press the Alt-F5 key combination immediately after making the entry.

To enter a time

1. Move the cell selector to the cell in which you want to enter the time.

2. Press **Ctrl-D**.

3. Type the date in one of these formats:

Format	Example
HH:MM:SS AM/PM	03:13:08 PM
HH:MM AM/PM	03:13 PM
HH:MM:SS	15:13:08 (24-hour clock)
HH:MM	15:13 (24-hour clock)

4. Press **Enter**.

Add cells

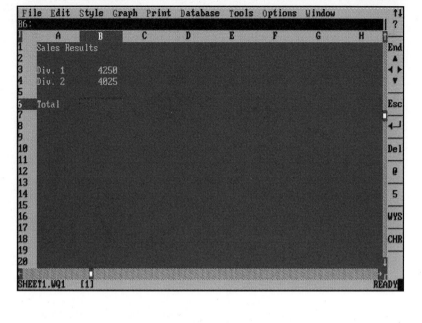

Oops!
If the formula is incorrect, you may have pointed to the wrong cells or included too many cells. Delete the entry and start over.

1. **Use the arrow keys to move the cell selector to cell B6.**

   Cell B6 will display the result of the calculation. You see `B6:` on the input line. The mode indicator displays `READY`, which tells you that Quattro Pro is ready for an entry.

2. **Type + (plus sign).**

   Typing + places you in `VALUE` mode and tells Quattro Pro that you want to enter a formula. To add the contents of two or more cells, you create an addition formula. You point to the cells that you want to include in this formula.

3. **Press the ↑ key three times.**

   Pressing the ↑ key three times moves the cell selector to cell B3. This is the first cell that you want to include in the addition formula. You see `+B3` on the input line.

4. **Type + (plus sign).**

   The + is the operator. It tells Quattro Pro which mathematical operation you want to perform. In this case, you are performing addition. The cell selector returns to B6.

5. **Press the ↑ key twice.**

   Pressing the ↑ key twice moves the cell selector to cell B4. This is the second cell that you want to include. You see `+B3+B4` on the input line.

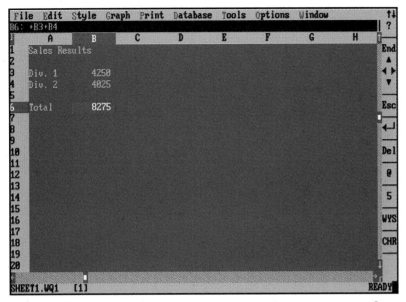

after

6. **Press Enter.**

   Pressing Enter tells Quattro Pro that you are finished with the
   addition formula. You see the results of the formula (8275) in
   cell B6. On the input line, you see the formula (+B3+B4).

Why use a formula?
A formula references a
cell's contents, not a fixed
value. Therefore, when
you change the values in
cells, the formula's result
is recalculated
automatically.

REVIEW

1. Move the cell selector to the cell in which you want to
   enter the formula.

2. Type +.

3. Type or point to the first value that you want to add.

4. Type +.

5. Type or point to the second value that you want to add.

6. Continue typing + and pointing to values until you
   include all the cells that you want.

7. Press **Enter**.

To add cells

Use the @SUM function
You also can use the
@SUM function to add
values. See *TASK: Total
cells with the @SUM
function.*

Subtract cells

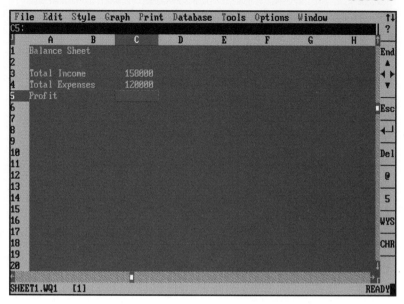

Oops!
If the formula is incorrect, you may have pointed to the wrong cells or included too many cells. Delete the formula and start over.

1. **Use the arrow keys to move the cell selector to cell C5.**

   Cell C5 will display the result of the calculation. You see `C5:` on the input line. The mode indicator displays `READY`, which tells you that Quattro Pro is ready for an entry.

2. **Type + (plus sign).**

   Typing + places you in `VALUE` mode and tells Quattro Pro that you want to enter a formula. You select the cells that you want the formula to include.

3. **Press the ↑ key twice.**

   Pressing the ↑ key twice moves the cell selector to cell C3. This is the first cell that you want to include in the formula. You see `+C3` on the input line.

4. **Type – (minus sign).**

   The – is the operator. This tells Quattro Pro which mathematical operation you are performing. In this case, you want to perform subtraction. You see `+C3-` on the input line. The cell selector returns to C5.

5. **Press the ↑ key once.**

   Pressing the ↑ key once moves the cell selector to cell C4. This is the second cell that you want to include. You see `+C3-C4` on the input line.

Easy **Quattro Pro**

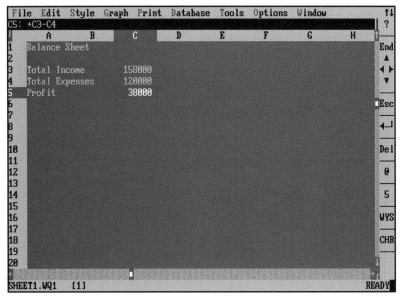

after

6. Press **Enter**.

   Pressing Enter tells Quattro Pro that you are finished with the formula. You see the results of the formula (38000) in cell C5. On the input line, you see the formula (+C3-C4).

1. Move the cell selector to the cell in which you want to enter the subtraction formula.

2. Type +.

3. Type or point to the first value you want to include.

4. Type –.

5. Type or point to the second value.

6. Continue typing – and pointing to values until you include all the ones that you want.

7. Press **Enter**.

To subtract cells

Delete an entry
To delete an entry, press the Alt-F5 key combination immediately after typing the entry.

Why use a formula?
A formula references a cell's contents, not a fixed value. Therefore, when you change the values in cells, the formula's result is recalculated automatically.

Entering and Editing Data

Multiply cells

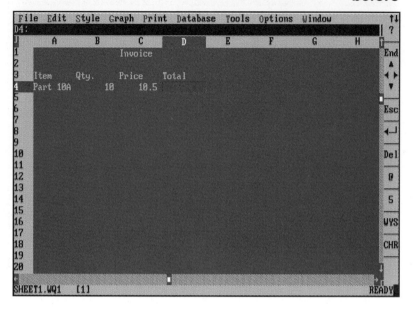

Oops!
If the formula is incorrect, you may have pointed to the wrong cells or included too many cells. Delete the entry and start over.

1. **Use the arrow keys to move the cell selector to cell D4.**

   Cell D4 will display the result of the calculation. You see D4: on the input line. The mode indicator displays READY, which tells you that Quattro Pro is ready for an entry.

2. **Type + (plus sign).**

   Typing + places you in VALUE mode and tells Quattro Pro that you want to enter a formula.

3. **Press the ← key twice.**

   Pressing the ← key twice moves the cell selector to cell B4. This is the first cell that you want to include in the formula. You see +B4 on the input line.

4. **Press * (asterisk).**

   The * is the operator. This tells Quattro Pro which mathematical operation you want to perform. In this case, you want to perform multiplication. You see +B4* on the input line. The cell selector returns to cell D4.

5. **Press the ← key once.**

   Pressing the ← key once moves the cell selector to cell C4. This is the second cell that you want to include in the formula. You see +B4*C4 on the input line.

Easy **Quattro Pro**

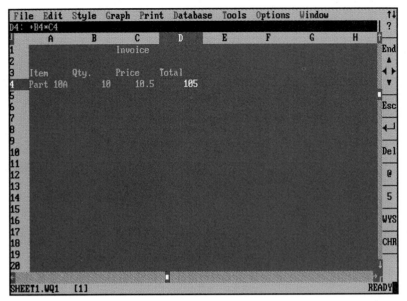

File Edit Style Graph Print Database Tools Options Window   ↑↓
D4: +B4*C4   ?
       A   B   C   D   E   F   G   H   End
1   Invoice   ▲
2   ◄ ►
3   Item   Qty.   Price   Total   ▼
4   Part 10A   10   10.5   105
5   Esc
6
7   ◄┘
8
9
10   Del
11
12   @
13
14   5
15
16   WYS
17
18   CHR
19
20
SHEET1.WQ1   [1]   READY

after

6. **Press Enter.**

Pressing Enter tells Quattro Pro that you are finished with the
formula. You see the results of the formula (105) in cell D4. On the
input line, you see the formula (+B4*C4).

Delete an entry
To delete an entry,
press the Alt-F5 key
combination immediately
after typing the entry.

To multiply cells

1. Move the cell selector to the cell in which you want to
   enter the multiplication formula.

2. Type +.

3. Type or point to the first value that you want to include.

4. Type *.

5. Type or point to the second value.

6. Continue typing * and pointing to values until you
   include all the values that you want.

7. Press **Enter**.

Why use a formula?
A formula references a
cell's contents, not a fixed
value. Therefore, when
you change the values in
cells, the formula's result
is recalculated
automatically.

Divide two cells

```
 File  Edit  Style  Graph  Print  Database  Tools  Options  Window        ↑↓
C5:                                                                         ?
        A         B         C         D         E         F         G         H
1  Log Sheet                                                              End
2                                                                          ▲
3  Finished Chapters        12                                           ◄ ►
4  Total Chapters           36                                             ▼
5  Percent Done
6                                                                        ▪Esc
7
8                                                                         ◄┘
9
10                                                                        Del
11
12                                                                         @
13
14                                                                         5
15
16                                                                        WYS
17
18                                                                        CHR
19
20
SHEET1.WQ1   [1]                                                       READY
```

Oops!
If the formula is incorrect, you may have pointed to the wrong cells or you may have included too many cells. Delete the entry and start over.

1. **Use the arrow keys to move the cell selector to cell C5.**

   Cell C5 will display the result of the calculation. You see `C5:` on the input line. The mode indicator displays `READY`, which tells you that Quattro Pro is ready for an entry.

2. **Type + (plus sign).**

   Typing + places you in `VALUE` mode and tells Quattro Pro that you want to enter a formula.

3. **Press the ↑ key twice.**

   Pressing the ↑ key twice moves the cell selector to cell C3. This is the first cell that you want to include in the formula. You see `+C3` on the input line.

4. **Press the / (forward slash) key.**

   The / is the operator. This tells Quattro Pro which mathematical operation you want to perform. In this case, you want to perform division. The cell selector returns to C5.

5. **Press the ↑ key once.**

   Pressing the ↑ key once moves the cell selector to cell C4. This is the second cell that you want to include. You see `+C3/C4` on the input line.

Easy **Quattro Pro**

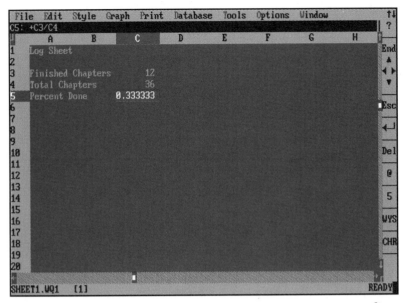

after

Delete an entry
To delete an entry,
press the Alt-F5 key
combination immediately
after typing it.

6. Press **Enter**.

Pressing Enter tells Quattro Pro that you are finished with the formula. You see the results of the formula (0.333333) in cell C5. On the input line, you see the formula (+C3/C4).

REVIEW

1. Move the cell selector to the cell in which you want to enter the division formula.

2. Type +.

3. Type or point to the first value that you want to include.

4. Type /.

5. Type or point to the second value.

6. Press **Enter**.

To divide two cells

Why use a formula?
A formula references a cell's contents, not a fixed value. Therefore, when you change the values in cells, the formula's result is recalculated automatically.

Overwrite a cell

before

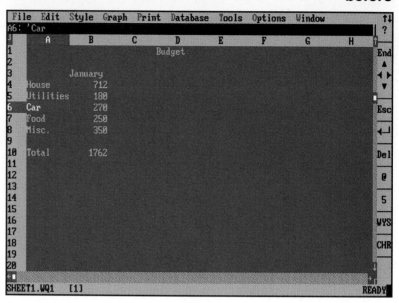

1. **Use the arrow keys to move the cell selector to cell A6.**

   A6 contains the entry that you want to overwrite. You see A6: on the input line, followed by the current entry, 'Car. The mode indicator displays READY, which tells you that Quattro Pro is ready for an entry.

2. **Type Auto.**

   Auto is the new entry for the cell.

3. **Press Enter.**

   Pressing Enter replaces the previous entry with the new entry.

64

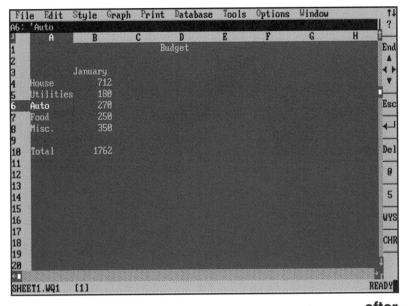

after

Be careful!
Do not overwrite formulas. If you type over a formula with a value, the formula will not be updated and the spreadsheet results may be incorrect.

1. Move the cell selector to the cell that you want to overwrite.

2. Type the new entry.

3. Press **Enter**.

To overwrite a cell

Edit a cell
If the change is minor or the entry is long, edit the cell instead. See *TASK: Edit a cell*.

Edit a cell

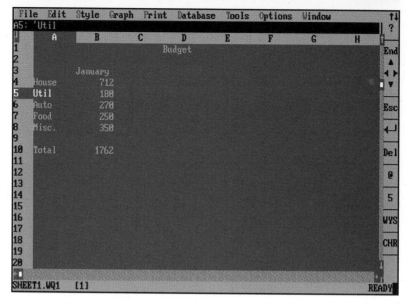

Oops!
While the cursor is still on the input line, you can press the Esc key to cancel the changes.

1. **Use the arrow keys to move the cell selector to cell A5.**

   A5 contains the entry that you want to change. You see A5: on the input line, followed by the current entry. The mode indicator displays READY, which tells you that Quattro Pro is ready for an entry.

2. **Press F2.**

   The F2 key is the Edit key. Pressing this key places you in EDIT mode and moves the cursor to the input line. The cursor is at the end of the entry.

   You can use the arrow keys to move the cursor to the characters that you want to change or delete. You also can use the Backspace and Del keys to delete characters.

Easy **Quattro Pro**

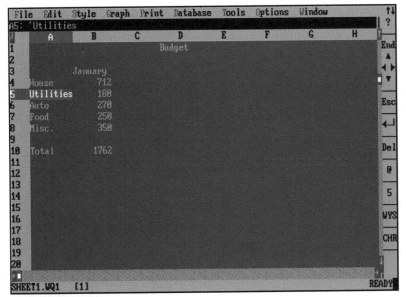

after

Restore the original entry
If you decide that you do not want the entry as you edited it, press the Alt-F5 key combination immediately after making the change.

3. Type **ities**.

   Typing *ities* changes the row label from Util to Utilities.

4. Press **Enter**.

   Pressing Enter accepts the new entry.

REVIEW

To edit a cell

1. Move the cell selector to the cell that you want to edit.

2. Press **F2** (Edit).

3. Edit the entry on the input line.

4. Press **Enter**.

Overwrite a cell
If the new entry is entirely different, overwrite the entry. See *TASK: Overwrite a cell*.

Erase a cell

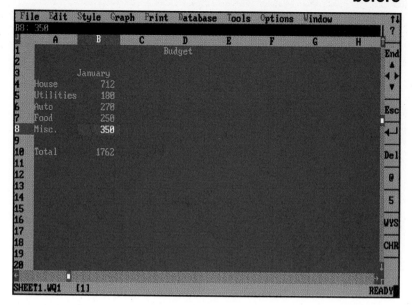

Oops!
To undo the deletion, press the Alt-F5 key combination immediately after erasing the cell contents.

1. **Use the arrow keys to move the cell selector to cell B8.**

   B8 is the cell that you want to erase. You see `B8:350` on the input line.

2. **Press Del.**

   Pressing the Del key removes the contents of cell B8.

Easy **Quattro Pro**

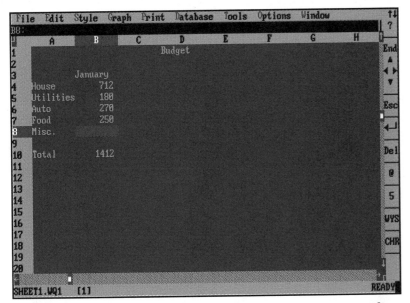

after

To erase a cell

1. Move the cell selector to the cell that you want to erase.

2. Press **Del**.

Copy a cell

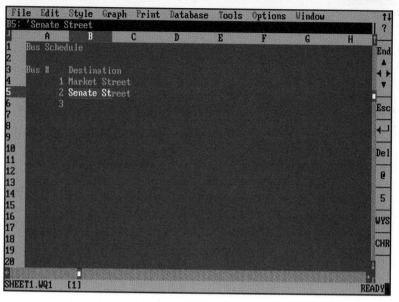

before

Oops!
To undo the copy, press the Alt-F5 key combination immediately after making the copy.

1. **Use the arrow keys to move the cell selector to cell B5.**

   B5 is the cell that you want to copy, or the *source cell*. You see B5: 'Senate Street on the input line. The mode indicator displays READY, which tells you that Quattro Pro is ready for an entry.

2. **Type /EC.**

   Typing /EC selects the Edit Copy command. You see the prompt Source block of cells: B5..B5. The mode indicator changes to POINT. In POINT mode, you can point to the cells that you want to include.

3. **Press Enter.**

   Pressing Enter confirms that you want to copy this cell. If you didn't select the cell in step 1, or if you want to select a different cell, you can type or point to the source cell before you press Enter.

   You see the prompt Destination for cells:B5. B5 is the current cell.

4. **Press the ↓ key once.**

   Pressing the ↓ key once moves the cell selector to cell B6. This is where you want the copy to appear.

70

Easy **Quattro Pro**

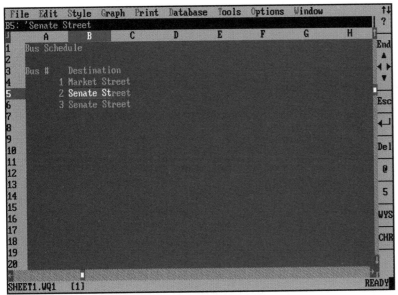

after

5. Press **Enter**.

Pressing Enter confirms the copy. The entry appears in both cells—B5 and B6. Quattro Pro copies the entry as well as the format (alignment, protection settings, and so on). See the section *Formatting the Spreadsheet* for more information on these settings.

The cell selector returns to cell B5.

1. Move the cell selector to the cell that you want to copy.

2. Press **/EC** to select the Edit Copy command.

3. Press **Enter**, or type or point to the correct source cell.

4. Move the cell selector to the cell in which you want the copy to appear.

5. Press **Enter**.

To copy a cell

Copy a block
You can also copy more than one cell (a block). See *TASK: Copy a block*.

Try a shortcut
Press the Ctrl-C key combination to select the Edit Copy command.

Entering and Editing Data

71

Move a cell

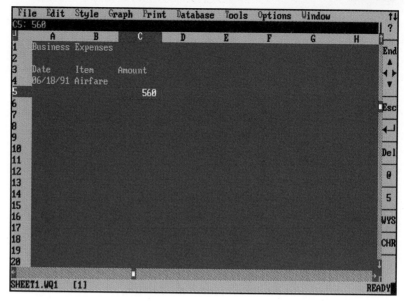

If you change your mind after selecting the source cell, press the Esc key until you return to the spreadsheet.

1. **Use the arrow keys to move the cell selector to cell C5.**

   C5 is the cell that you want to move, or the source cell. You see C5: 560 on the input line. The mode indicator displays READY, which tells you that Quattro Pro is ready for an entry.

2. **Type /EM.**

   Typing /EM selects the Edit Move command. You see the prompt Source block of cells: C5..C5 on the input line. The mode indicator displays POINT. In POINT mode, you can point to the cells that you want to move.

3. **Press Enter.**

   Pressing Enter confirms that this is the source cell. If you didn't select the cell or if you want to select a different cell, you can type or point to the source cell before you press Enter.

   You see the prompt Destination for cells: C5. C5 is the current cell.

4. **Press the ↑ key once.**

   Pressing the ↑ key once moves the cell selector to cell C4. This cell is the destination cell, which is the location where you want the entry to appear.

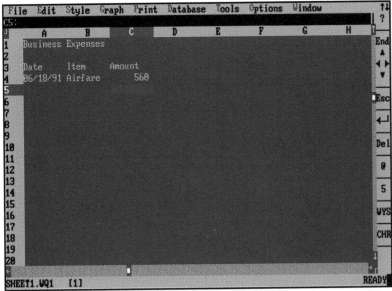

after

5. Press **Enter**.

Pressing Enter confirms the move. The entry is moved to cell C4 and the original cell (C5) is blank. The cell selector returns to C5.

---

1. Place the cell selector in the cell that you want to move.

2. Press **/EM** to select the Edit Move command.

3. Press **Enter**, or type or point to the correct source cell and press **Enter**.

4. Move the cell selector to the cell in which you want the entry to appear.

5. Press **Enter**.

**To move
a cell**

Reverse the move
To undo the move, press the Alt-F5 key combination immediately after moving the cell.

Try a shortcut
Press the Ctrl-M key combination to select the Edit Move command.

Go to a specific cell

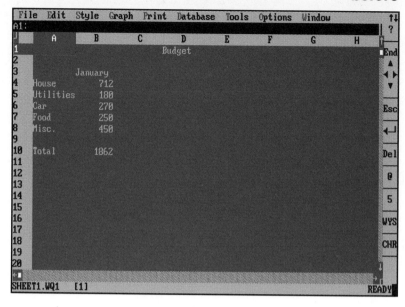

Oops!
To return to the first cell in the spreadsheet, press the Home key.

1. **Press F5.**

   The F5 key is the GoTo key. You see the prompt `Enter address to go to:` on the input line. The current cell also appears in the prompt. The mode indicator displays `POINT`.

2. **Type B10.**

   Typing *B10* tells Quattro Pro that you want the cell selector to go to cell B10.

3. **Press Enter.**

   When you press Enter, the cell selector moves to the cell that you indicated.

Easy **Quattro Pro**

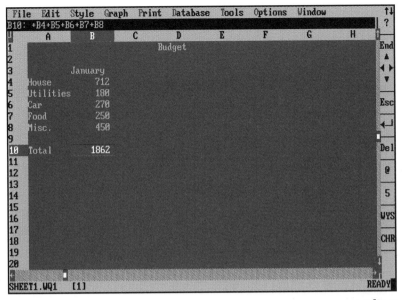

```
 File  Edit  Style  Graph  Print  Database  Tools  Options  Window        ↑↓
B10: +B4+B5+B6+B7+B8                                                        ?
U      A        B        C       D       E       F       G       H       End
1                        Budget                                            ▲
2                                                                        ◄ ►
3            January                                                       ▼
4  House       712
5  Utilities   180                                                       Esc
6  Car         270
7  Food        250                                                        ↵
8  Misc.       450
9                                                                        Del
10 Total      1862
11                                                                         @
12
13                                                                         5
14
15
16                                                                       WYS
17
18                                                                       CHR
19
20
SHEET1.WQ1   [1]                                                        READY
```

after

REVIEW

1. Press **F5** (GoTo).

2. Type the cell reference.

3. Press **Enter**.

To go to a specific cell

Use Undo

before

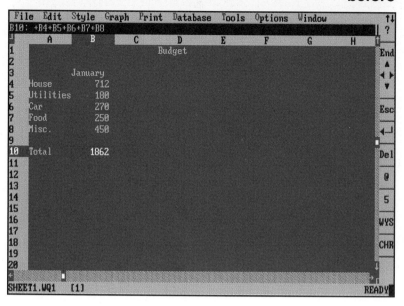

Oops!
To undo the "undo,"
press the Alt-F5 key
combination again.

1. **Use the arrow keys to move the cell selector to cell B10.**
   You will make an entry in cell B10 and then undo that entry. You see B10: on the input line, followed by the current entry.

2. **Type 2000.**
   2000 is the new text that you want to insert into the cell.

3. **Press Enter.**
   Pressing Enter overwrites the formula. When you edit the spreadsheet, however, you want to be sure not to overwrite formulas. Resulting figures may not be correct if the formula has been deleted.

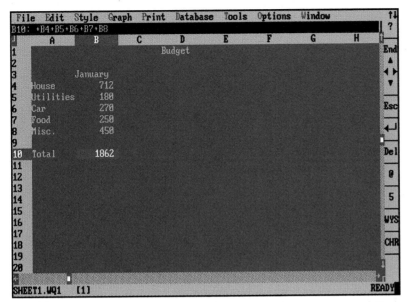

after

4. Press **Alt-F5**.

The Alt-F5 key combination is the Undo key combination. Pressing these keys returns the cell to its original form. Notice that the Before and After screens are the same because you have reversed any changes that you made to the spreadsheet.

Press **Alt-F5** (Undo).

What does Undo reverse?
Undo only undoes the last operation, and you can undo only certain tasks. See your Quattro Pro manual or *Using Quattro Pro 3,* Special Edition.

To use Undo

Turn on Undo
You must turn on Undo before you can use it. See *TASK: Turn on Undo.*

Managing Files

The section covers the following tasks:

Save a spreadsheet for the first time

Save a spreadsheet again

Save a spreadsheet with a new name

Abandon a spreadsheet

Erase a spreadsheet

Retrieve an existing spreadsheet

Create a new spreadsheet

Change the directory

Set the default directory

Delete a spreadsheet file

Save a spreadsheet for the first time

```
File  Edit  Style  Graph  Print  Database  Tools  Options  Window    ↑↓
A1: 'Sales                                                             ?
     A        B        C        D        E        F      G     H     ■End
1  Sales                                                                ▲
2            Qtr 1    Qtr 2    Qtr 3    Qtr 4                         ◄ ►
3  East       800      900      850      650                           ▼
4  West      1000     1250      790     1300
5  North     1450     1450     1550     1600                          Esc
6  South      500      700      650      980
7                                                                      ↵
8  Total    $3,750   $4,300   $3,840   $4,530
9                                                                      Del
10                                                                      @
11
12                                                                      5
13
14
15                                                                    WYS
16
17                                                                    CHR
18
19
20
■
SHEET1.WQ1   [1]                                              READY■
```

Oops!
If you type a file name that already exists, Quattro Pro warns you. Type C to cancel the operation. Start over, using a different file name.

1. **Type /FS.**

   Typing /FS selects the File Save command. The File Save dialog box appears with the prompt `Enter save file name:`. A list of file names that have already been saved appears in the dialog box.

2. **Type SALES.**

   SALES is the file name that you want to assign to the cell. You can type up to eight characters. As a general rule, use only alphanumeric characters. You do not have to enter an extension. Quattro Pro automatically adds the WQ1 extension. This entry, for example, would be called *SALES.WQ1*.

Easy **Quattro Pr**

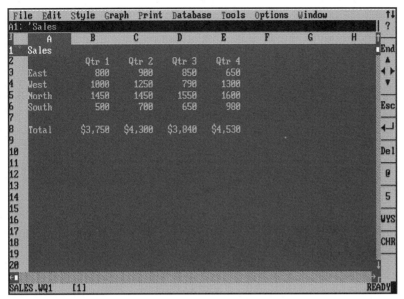

File	Edit	Style	Graph	Print	Database	Tools	Options	Window	↑↓

A1: 'Sales

	A	B	C	D	E	F	G	H	?
1	Sales								■End
2		Qtr 1	Qtr 2	Qtr 3	Qtr 4				▲
3	East	800	900	850	650				◄ ►
4	West	1000	1250	790	1300				▼
5	North	1450	1450	1550	1600				
6	South	500	700	650	980				Esc
7									
8	Total	$3,750	$4,300	$3,840	$4,530				↵
9									
10									Del
11									
12									@
13									
14									5
15									
16									WYS
17									
18									CHR
19									
20									

SALES.WQ1   [1]   READY

after

3. Press **Enter**.

You return to the spreadsheet. On the status line, you see the file name SALES.WQ1.

1. Type **/FS** to select the File Save command.

2. Type the file name.

3. Press **Enter**.

To save a spreadsheet for the first time

Be careful!
Until you save a spreadsheet, the data is not committed to disk. You can lose the data if you have a power loss.

Try a shortcut
Press the Ctrl-S key combination to select the File Save command.

Managing Files

81

Save a spreadsheet again

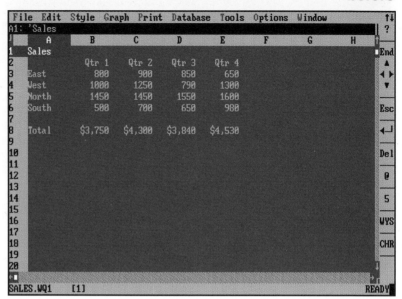

Oops!
If you don't want to replace the original version, type C to cancel the command.

1. **Type /FS.**

   Typing /FS selects the File Save command. Because you have already named the file, you are not prompted for a file name. Instead, you see the prompt `File already exists: Cancel, Replace, Backup.` You see this prompt in the After Screen.

2. **Type R.**

   Typing R selects Replace. The on-screen version of the file is saved to disk and replaces the original version.

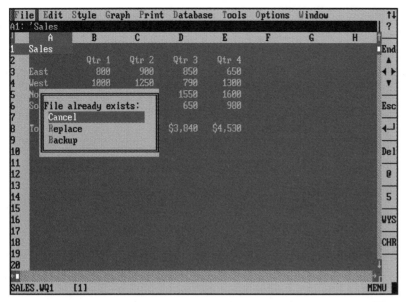

after

**Keep two versions
of a file**
If you want to keep both
versions—the on-screen
version and the original—
you can use the File Save
As command. See *TASK:
Save a spreadsheet with
a new name.*

REVIEW

1. Type **/FS** to select the File Save command.

2. Type **R** to select Replace.

To save a spreadsheet again

Try a shortcut
Press the Ctrl-S key
combination to select the
File Save command.

Managing Files

83

TASK

Save a spreadsheet with a new name

before

```
 File  Edit  Style  Graph  Print  Database  Tools  Options  Window        ↑↓
A1: 'Sales                                                                  ?
      A        B        C        D        E        F        G        H    ■End
1   Sales                                                                   ▲
2            Qtr 1    Qtr 2    Qtr 3    Qtr 4                              ◄ ►
3   East      800      900      850      650                                ▼
4   West     1000     1250      790     1300
5   North    1450     1450     1550     1600                               Esc
6   South     500      700      650      980
7                                                                          ←┘
8   Total   $3,750   $4,300   $3,840   $4,530
9                                                                          Del
10
11                                                                          @
12
13                                                                          5
14
15
16                                                                         WYS
17
18                                                                         CHR
19
20
SALES.WQ1    [1]                                                         READY
```

Oops!
If you don't want two copies of the same spreadsheet, delete the one that you don't want. See *TASK: Delete a spreadsheet file.*

1. Type /FA.

Typing /FA selects the File Save As command. This command enables you to specify a different name for the file. The File Save As dialog box appears. You see the prompt Enter save file name:. The current drive, path, and file name appear after this prompt.

2. Type SALES91.

SALES91 is the file name that you want to assign. The file name can be up to eight characters long. As a general rule, use only alphanumeric characters. You do not have to type an extension. Quattro Pro automatically adds the WQ1 extension. This file name, for example, would be *SALES91.WQ1*.

84

Easy **Quattro Pr**

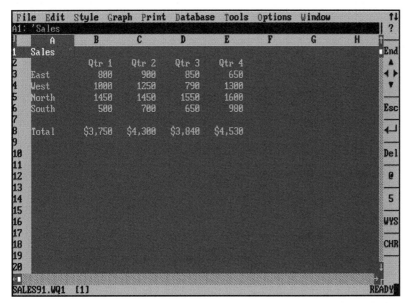

after

3. Press **Enter**.

Pressing Enter confirms the save and returns you to the spreadsheet. You see the new file name on the status line. The original spreadsheet remains on disk, intact.

1. Type **/FA** to select the File Save As command.

2. Type the new file name.

3. Press **Enter**.

Create a template
You can use this command to create one spreadsheet as a template for a series of similar spreadsheets. Then open the template, make changes, and save it with a different name.

Managing Files

85

Abandon a spreadsheet

```
File  Edit  Style  Graph  Print  Database  Tools  Options  Window        ↑↓
C8: 450                                                                    ?
      A        B        C        D        E        F        G        H    
1                          Budget                                        End
2                                                                         ▲
3                 Jan      Feb                                          ◄  ►
4    House        712      712                                           ▼
5    Utilities    180      190                                          
6    Car          270      325                                          Esc
7    Food         250      300                                          
8    Misc.        350      450                                          ↵
9                                                                        
10   Total        1762     1977                                         Del
11                                                                       
12                                                                       @
13                                                                       
14                                                                       5
15                                                                       
16                                                                       WYS
17                                                                       
18                                                                       CHR
19                                                                       
20                                                                       
SHEET1.WQ1   [1]                                                       READY
```

Oops!

If you don't want to abandon the spreadsheet, type N in step 2. Then save the spreadsheet.

1. **Type /FE.**

   Typing /FE selects the File Erase command. If you have made any changes, you see a dialog box that asks `Lose your changes?`. You have two choices: No or Yes.

2. **Type Y.**

   Typing Y tells Quattro Pro that you do not want to save the changes. The spreadsheet is closed, and a new blank spreadsheet appears on-screen.

Easy **Quattro Pro**

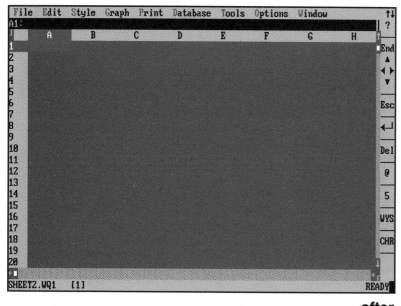

| File | Edit | Style | Graph | Print | Database | Tools | Options | Window | ↑↓ |

A1:

| | A | B | C | D | E | F | G | H | |

after

1. Type **/FE** to select the File Erase command.

2. Type **Y**.

To abandon a spreadsheet

Erase a spreadsheet

Oops!
Use the File Retrieve command to reopen a closed spreadsheet. See *TASK: Retrieve an existing spreadsheet*.

before

```
File  Edit  Style  Graph  Print  Database  Tools  Options  Window        ↑↓
C10: @SUM(C4..C8)                                                          ?
      A        B        C        D      E       F      G      H          End
1                            Budget                                       ▲
2                                                                        ◄ ►
3              Jan      Feb                                               ▼
4   House      712      712
5   Utilities  180      190
6   Car        270      325                                              Esc
7   Food       250      300
8   Misc.      350      345                                              ◄┘
9
10  Total      1762     1872                                             Del
11
12                                                                        @
13
14                                                                        5
15
16                                                                       WYS
17
18                                                                       CHR
19
20
SHEET1.WQ1   [1]                                                        READY
```

1. **Save the spreadsheet.**

   To complete this step, see any of the tasks that discuss saving the spreadsheet.

2. **Type /FE.**

   Typing /FE selects the File Erase command. The spreadsheet is erased, or closed. Note that the spreadsheet is erased from memory and from the screen; it is not erased from disk. You can use File Retrieve to open the closed spreadsheet if you saved it.

   A new blank spreadsheet appears on-screen. Quattro Pro assigns the new spreadsheet the default name SHEET, followed by a number. It would name the first blank spreadsheet, for example, SHEET1.

Easy **Quattro Pro**

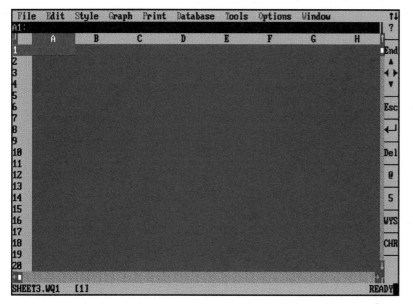

| File | Edit | Style | Graph | Print | Database | Tools | Options | Window | ↑↓ |

A1:

| | A | B | C | D | E | F | G | H | | ? |

1 ... End
2 ... ▲
3 ... ◄ ►
4 ... ▼
5
6 ... Esc
7
8 ... ←┘
9
10 ... Del
11
12 ... @
13
14 ... 5
15
16 ... WYS
17
18 ... CHR
19
20

SHEET3.WQ1   [1]   READY

after

Did you save the spreadsheet?
If you have unsaved changes to the spreadsheet, Quattro Pro prompts you. Type Y to abandon the changes or N to return to the spreadsheet.

REVIEW

1. Save the spreadsheet.

2. Type /FE to select the File Erase command.

To erase a spreadsheet

Use the File Close command
You also can use the File Close command to close the spreadsheet. See *Using Quattro Pro 3*, Special Edition.

Retrieve an existing spreadsheet

before

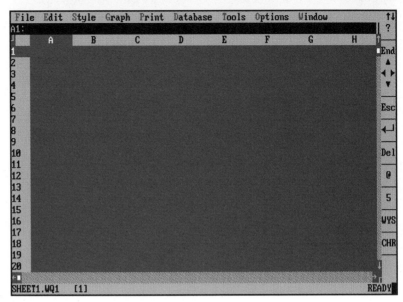

Oops!
If you retrieve the wrong spreadsheet, erase the spreadsheet and try again. See *TASK: Erase a spreadsheet*.

1. Save the current spreadsheet.

To complete this step, see any of the tasks that discuss saving the spreadsheet. When you retrieve a spreadsheet, the current spreadsheet is erased from memory. Be sure to save the current spreadsheet before you begin working on another one.

If you have just started Quattro Pro and have a blank spreadsheet on-screen, you do not have to complete this step.

2. Type /FR.

Typing /FR selects the File Retrieve command. You see the prompt `Enter name of file to retrieve:`. You also see a list of existing file names in the current directory.

3. Type SALES.

SALES is the name of the file that you want to retrieve. You can type the file name, or you can point to the file name using the mouse or the arrow keys. If you do not have a file named SALES, select one that you do have.

Easy **Quattro Pro**

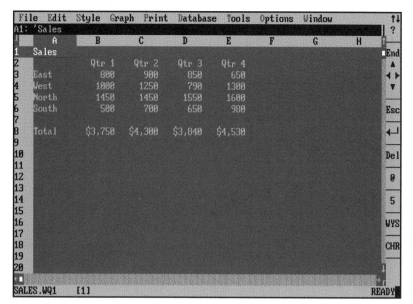

Use the File Open command
You can use the File Open command to open a spreadsheet and leave the current spreadsheet open. See *Using Quattro Pro 3*, Special Edition.

4. Press **Enter**.

Pressing Enter confirms that you want to retrieve the highlighted file. The spreadsheet is retrieved and appears on-screen. The file name appears in the status line.

REVIEW

To retrieve an existing spreadsheet

1. Type **/FR** to select the File Retrieve command.

2. Type or point to the file name.

3. Press **Enter**.

Create a new spreadsheet

```
 File  Edit  Style  Graph  Print  Database  Tools  Options  Window        ↑↓
A1: 'Sales                                                                  ?
      A       B       C       D       E       F       G       H          ■End
1   Sales                                                                   ▲
2           Qtr 1   Qtr 2   Qtr 3   Qtr 4                                  ◄ ►
3   East      800     900     850     650                                   ▼
4   West     1000    1250     790    1300
5   North    1450    1450    1550    1600                                  Esc
6   South     500     700     650     980
7                                                                           ↵
8   Total  $3,750  $4,300  $3,840  $4,530
9                                                                          Del
10
11                                                                          0
12
13                                                                          5
14
15
16                                                                        WYS
17
18                                                                        CHR
19
20
SALES.WQ1    [1]                                                        READY
```

Oops!
If you don't want to create a new spreadsheet after all, abandon the new spreadsheet. See *TASK: Abandon a spreadsheet*.

1. **Close the current spreadsheet.**
   See *TASK: Erase a spreadsheet* for help with this step. You can have more than one spreadsheet open, but you should get into the habit of saving and closing spreadsheets after you finish working on them.

2. **Type /FN.**
   Typing /FN selects the File New command. A blank spreadsheet appears on-screen.

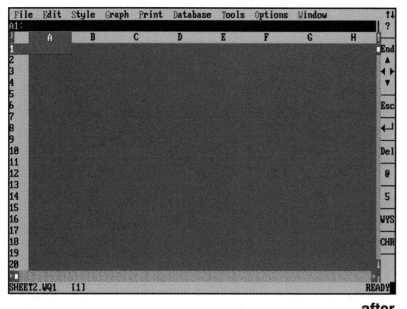

| File | Edit | Style | Graph | Print | Database | Tools | Options | Window | ↑↓ |

A1:

| | A | B | C | D | E | F | G | H | ? |

1 ■End
2 ▲
3 ◄ ►
4 ▼
5
6
7 Esc
8
9 ↵
10
11 Del
12
13 @
14
15 5
16
17 WYS
18
19 CHR
20

SHEET2.WQ1   [1]   READY

after

Save your spreadsheet
Remember to save your new spreadsheet after you enter data into it. See *TASK: Save a spreadsheet for the first time.*

REVIEW

1. Close the current spreadsheet.

2. Type /**FN** to select the File New command.

To create a new spreadsheet

Change the directory

before

```
File  Edit  Style  Graph  Print  Database  Tools  Options  Window        ↑↓
                                                                           ?
  New                                    E     F     G     H
  Open                                                                    End
  Retrieve                                                                 ▲
                                                                          ◄ ►
  Save                          Ctrl-S                                     ▼
  Save As        C:\EZQP\SHEET1.WQ1
  Save All                                                                Esc
  Close
  Close All                                                                ↵
  Erase
                                                                          Del
  Directory              C:\QPRO\
  Work                                                                     @
  Util Enter name of directory:
  Exit C:\QPRO                                                             5

  1                                                                       WYS
  17
  18              Enter          Esc                                      CHR
  19
  20
Set a temporary data directory                                     EDIT
```

Oops!
If you want to use a different directory, follow this same procedure to change the directory again.

1. **Type /FD**.

   Typing /FD selects the File Directory command. You see the prompt `Enter name of directory:`. The name of the current drive and directory appear after the prompt.

2. **Type DATA**.

   DATA is the directory that you want to use. If you haven't created this directory, type the name of a directory that you have created.

3. **Press Enter**.

   Pressing Enter confirms the new directory name. Now when you use any of the File commands, Quattro Pro uses this directory. That is, Quattro Pro lists the files in this directory and saves any new files to this directory.

Easy **Quattro Pro**

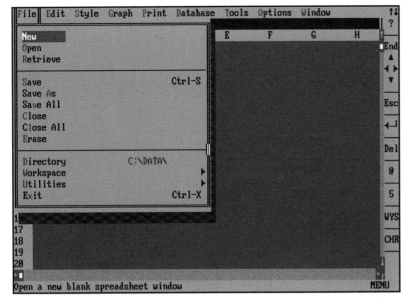

| File | Edit | Style | Graph | Print | Database | Tools | Options | Window | ↑↓ |

```
File  Edit  Style  Graph  Print  Database  Tools  Options  Window    ↑↓
                                                                      ?
New                               E        F        G        H      ■End
Open                                                                  ▲
Retrieve                                                             ◄ ►
                                                                      ▼
Save                   Ctrl-S
Save As                                                              Esc
Save All
Close                                                                ◄┘
Close All
Erase                                                               Del

Directory              C:\DATA\                                      @
Workspace                        ►
Utilities                        ►                                   5
Exit                   Ctrl-X
                                                                    WYS
1
17                                                                  CHR
18
19
20
◄                                                                ▼
Open a new blank spreadsheet window                               MENU
```

after

Notice that this file is the directory for this work session only. If you quit and restart the program, the default directory is used. To set the default directory, see *TASK: Set the default directory*.

4. **Type /F.**

   Typing /F opens the File menu. You see the new directory listed next to `Directory`.

5. **Press Esc.**

   Pressing the Esc key closes the menu.

1. Type **/FD** to select the File Directory command.

2. Type the new directory name.

3. Press **Enter.**

To change the directory

Create a directory
You must create a directory before you use the File Directory command. See your DOS manual for more information.

Set the default directory

before

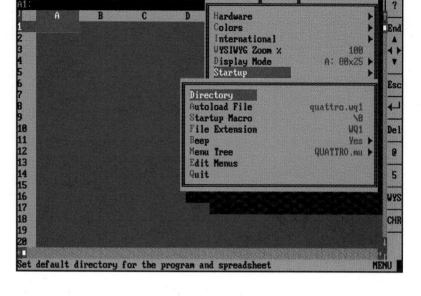

Oops!
If the procedure didn't work, follow the steps again and be sure to type U to update the settings.

1. Type /OS.

Typing /OS selects the Options Startup command. You see a list of startup options that you can specify. For complete information on all options, see the Quattro Pro manual or *Using Quattro Pro 3*, Special Edition.

2. Type D.

Typing D selects Directory from the menu. You see the prompt Directory at startup.

3. Type C:\DATA.

Typing C:\DATA sets the DATA directory as the default.

4. Press Enter.

Pressing Enter confirms your choice. The new directory is listed next to the menu item.

5. Type Q.

Typing Q closes the menu.

6. Type U.

Typing U selects Update. You must select this command to update the settings. If you don't type U, the settings are not saved.

Now when you start the program, Quattro Pro uses this directory to list and save files.

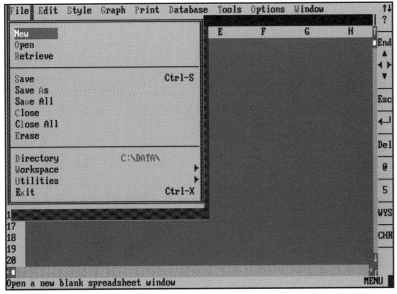

after

Create a directory
You must create a directory before you use the File Directory command. See your DOS manual for more information.

7. Type **Q**.

Typing Q closes the Options menu.

8. Type **/F**.

Typing /F opens the File menu. Notice that the new directory is listed.

9. Press **Esc**.

Pressing the Esc key closes the menu.

R E V I E W

To set the default directory

1. Type **/OSD** to select the Options Startup Directory command.

2. Type the directory name.

3. Press **Enter**.

4. Type **Q** to select Quit.

5. Type **U** to select Update.

6. Type **Q** to select Quit.

Delete a spreadsheet file

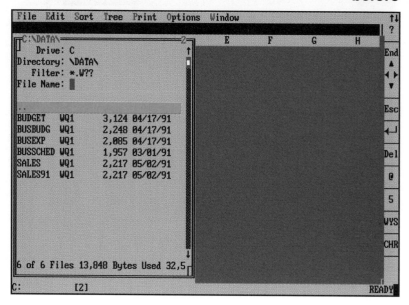

Oops!
If you are not positive that you want to erase a file, type N in step 5. *You cannot undelete a file with Quattro Pro.*

1. **Type /FU.**

   Typing /FU selects the File Utilities command. You see a menu with these choices: DOS Shell, File Manager, and SQZ!

2. **Type F.**

   Typing F selects File Manager from the list of choices. Notice that the Before screen shows the File Manager display.

3. **Use the arrow keys to highlight SALES91.**

   SALES91 is the spreadsheet that you want to delete. You see a check mark next to this file.

4. **Type /EE.**

   Typing /EE selects the Edit Erase command. You see the prompt
   Are you sure you want to delete this file?

5. **Type Y.**

   Typing Y deletes the file. The name is removed from the file list.

6. **Type /FC.**

   Typing /FC closes the File Manager.

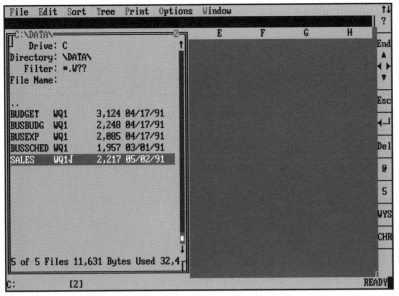

File Edit Sort Tree Print Options Window   ↑↓
                                                                   ?
C:\DATA\─────────────────────2─┐   E   F   G   H   ┌─ End
    Drive: C   ↑   │   ▲
Directory: \DATA\   │ ◄ ►
   Filter: *.W??   │   ▼
File Name: │
                                                           │ Esc
..   │
BUDGET   WQ1   3,124 04/17/91   │ ←┘
BUSBUDG   WQ1   2,248 04/17/91   │
BUSEXP   WQ1   2,085 04/17/91   │ Del
BUSSCHED WQ1   1,957 03/01/91   │
SALES   WQ1√   2,217 05/02/91   │   @
                                                           │
                                                           │   5
                                                           │
                                                           │ WYS
                                                           │
                                                           │ CHR
                                                           │
5 of 5 Files 11,631 Bytes Used 32,4   └─
C: [2]   READY

after

What is the File Manager?
The File Manager program lets you perform extra functions, such as create directories, sort files, and copy files. See the Quattro Pro manual or *Using Quattro Pro 3*, Special Edition.

R E V I E W

To delete a spreadsheet file

1. Type /FU to select the File Utilities command.

2. Type F to open the File Manager program.

3. Highlight the file name that you want to delete.

4. Type /EE to select Edit Erase.

5. Type Y.

6. Type /FC to close the File Manager.

Formatting the Spreadsheet

This section covers the following tasks:

Set column width

Select a block

Center a block

Right-justify a block

Display dollar signs

Display commas

Display percent signs

Format a date

Format a time

Insert a row

Delete a row

Insert a column

Delete a column

Hide columns

Set column width

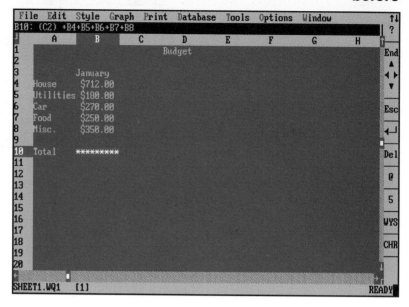

Oops!
To reset the width to the original setting, type /SR to select the Style Reset Width command.

1. **Use the arrow keys to move the cell selector to cell B10.**

   B10 is the cell for which you want to set the column width. The cell currently displays asterisks. When you see asterisks in a cell, it means that the column is not wide enough to display the results. Formatting often makes the entry longer than the default column width. For example, *712* is only three characters long. If you format the number as currency with two decimal places, however, the number appears as *$712.00*. This entry takes seven spaces. (Cell B10 has been formatted. For information on formatting, see other tasks in this section.)

   You can place the cell selector in any cell in the column that you want to change.

2. **Type /SC.**

   Typing /SC selects the Style Column Width command. You see the prompt `Alter the width of the current column [1..254]: 9`. The default column width is 9. You can enter any number from 1 to 254.

3. **Type 12.**

   Typing 12 sets the column width to 12 spaces.

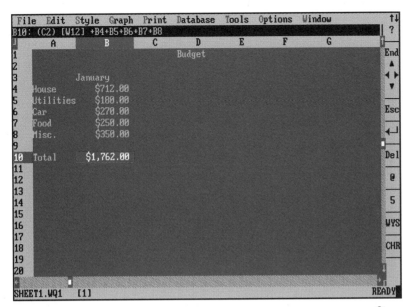

```
File  Edit  Style  Graph  Print  Database  Tools  Options  Window        ↑↓
B10: (C2) [W12] +B4+B5+B6+B7+B8                                           ?
     A            B          C        D        E        F        G        ▯
1                         Budget                                        End
2                                                                         ▲
3            January                                                    ◀ ▶
4    House        $712.00                                                 ▼
5    Utilities    $180.00
6    Car          $270.00                                               Esc
7    Food         $250.00
8    Misc.        $350.00                                                ↵
9
10   Total      $1,762.00                                               Del
11                                                                        @
12
13                                                                        5
14
15
16                                                                      WYS
17
18                                                                      CHR
19
20
SHEET1.WQ1    [1]                                              READY
```

after

4. Press **Enter**.

Pressing Enter widens the column to the specified number of spaces. If some cells still display asterisks, you need to widen the column even more.

You can tell that the column width has been changed by looking at the input line. For all entries in this column, you see [W12], which tells you that the width has been set to 12.

Widen columns with the mouse
You also can adjust column width with a mouse. Click on the column letter, press and hold the mouse button, and drag the mouse until the column is as wide or narrow as you want. Release the mouse button.

REVIEW

- 1. Move the cell selector to the column that you want to change.

2. Type **/SC** to select the Style Column Width command.

3. Type the new width or press the ← or → key to adjust width visually.

4. Press **Enter**.

To set column width

Try a shortcut
You can press the Ctrl-W key combination to select the Style Column Width command.

Formatting the Spreadsheet

Select a block

before

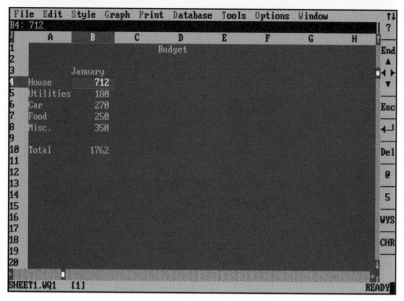

Oops!
To exit EXT mode, press
the Esc key; then press
any arrow key.

1. **Use the arrow keys to move the cell selector to cell B4.**

   B4 is the first cell in the block that you want to select.

2. **Press Shift-F7.**

   Shift-F7 is the Select key combination. Use this key combination to
   select (extend) a block. The status indicator displays EXT.

3. **Press the ↓ key six times.**

   Pressing the ↓ key six times selects the block from B4 to B10.

   After you select the block, you can perform other actions, such as
   formatting, moving, or copying the block. See the other tasks in
   this section for more information.

Easy **Quattro Pro**

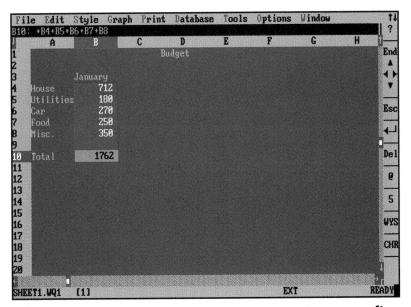

after

What is a block?
A block is any rectangular area of the spreadsheet, such as a cell, a column, a row, or several contiguous columns and rows.

To select a block

1. Move the cell selector to the first cell in the block that you want to select.

2. Press **Shift-F7** (Select).

3. Use the arrow keys to highlight the block.

4. Perform the block operation, such as format, move, copy, delete, and so on.

Select a block with the mouse
You also can select a block with a mouse. Click on the first cell of the block. Press and hold the mouse button and drag the mouse over the rest of the block. Release the mouse button.

Formatting the Spreadsheet

Center a block

```
File  Edit  Style  Graph  Print  Database  Tools  Options  Window        ↑↓
A3: 'Date                                                                 ?
       A        B        C        D        E        F        G       H
1                     Invoice Report                                     End
2                                                                         ▲
3     Date     Invoice  Price                                           ◄► ►
4     06/18/91     100  1259.99                                           ▼
5     07/16/91     180  1600.88
6                                                                        Esc
7
8                                                                        ◄┘
9
10                                                                       Del
11
12                                                                        @
13
14                                                                        5
15
16                                                                       WYS
17
18                                                                       CHR
19
20
SHEET1.WQ1    [1]                                                       READY
```

Oops!
To undo the alignment change, select the block, type /SA to select the Style Alignment command, and select a new alignment. The Alt-F5 key combination does not undo centering.

1. **Use the arrow keys to move the cell selector to cell A3.**

   A3 is the first cell in the block that you want to center. You see A3: followed by the current entry on the input line. Notice that the entry for this cell is preceded by an apostrophe. This character is the default prefix and indicates a label and left alignment.

2. **Press Shift-F7.**

   Shift-F7 is the Select key combination. You use this key combination to select the block that you want. The status indicator displays EXT.

3. **Press the → key twice.**

   Pressing the → key twice highlights the block A3..C3. This is the block that you want to center.

4. **Type /SA.**

   Typing /SA selects the Style Alignment command. You see a menu of alignment options: General, Left, Right, and Center.

Easy **Quattro Pro**

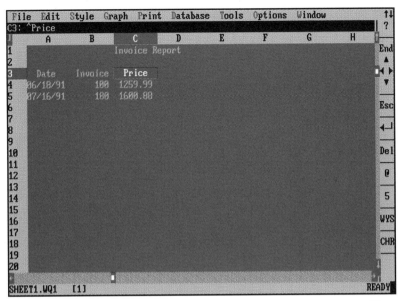

after

Center an entry
manually
To center an entry
manually, type ^ (caret)
and then type the entry.

5. Type **C**.

Typing C selects Center. Each entry in the block is centered in its cell. The cell selector remains in cell C3. Notice that on the input line, the entry appears as ^Price. The caret (^) is the centering prefix.

R E V I E W

1. Select the block that you want to center.

2. Type **/SAC** to select the Style Alignment Center command.

To center a block

Try a shortcut
You can press the Ctrl-A
key combination to select
the Style Alignment
command.

Right-justify a block

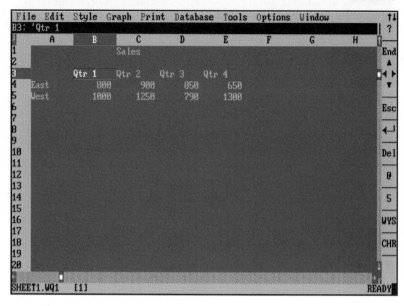

Oops!
To undo the alignment change, select the block, type /SA, and select a new alignment. The Alt-A5 key combination does not undo right-justification.

1. **Use the arrow keys to move the cell selector to cell B3.**

   B3 is the first cell in the block that you want to right-justify. You see `B3:` and the current entry on the input line. Notice that this entry is preceded by an apostrophe. The apostrophe is the default prefix and indicates a label and left alignment.

2. **Press Shift-F7.**

   Shift-F7 is the Select key combination. The status indicator displays `EXT`.

3. **Press the → key three times.**

   Pressing the → key three times selects the block B3..E3. This is the block that you want to right-justify.

4. **Type /SA.**

   Typing /SA selects the Style Alignment command. You see a menu of alignment choices: General, Left, Right, and Center.

Easy **Quattro Pro**

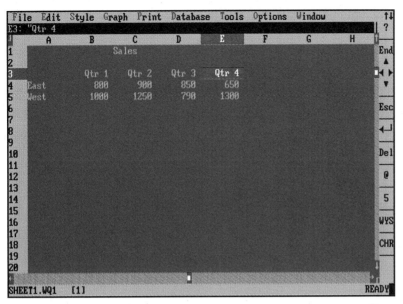

after

Right-justify an entry manually
To right-justify an entry manually, type " and then type the entry.

5. Type **R**.

   Typing R selects Right from the list. The entries in the cells are now right-justified.

   The cell selector remains in cell E3. Notice that on the input line the entry appears as "Qtr 4. The quotation mark (") is the right-justify prefix.

REVIEW

1. Select the block that you want to right-justify.

2. Type **/SAR** to select the Style Alignment Right command.

To right-justify a block

Try a shortcut
You can also press the Ctrl-A key combination to select the Style Alignment command.

Display dollar signs

```
File  Edit  Style  Graph  Print  Database  Tools  Options  Window        ↑↓
B4: 6.99                                                                  ?
       A        B        C      D      E      F      G      H           End
1   Inventory List                                                       ▲
2                                                                       ◄ ►
3   Stock #   Price                                                      ▼
4      100      6.99                                                     □
5      101     12.5                                                     Esc
6      102     13.99                                                    ◄┘
7      103      7.5
8                                                                      Del
9
10                                                                      @
11
12                                                                      5
13
14
15                                                                     WYS
16
17                                                                     CHR
18
19
20
SHEET1.WQ1   [1]                                                      READY
```

Oops!
To undo the formatting change, select the block, type /SN, and then select a new format or type R to reset. Alt-F5 will not undo the format change.

1. **Use the arrow keys to move the cell selector to cell B4.**
   B4 is the first cell in the block that you want to change.

2. **Press Shift-F7.**
   Shift-F7 is the Select key combination. The status indicator displays EXT.

3. **Press the ↓ key three times.**
   Pressing the ↓ key three times highlights the block B4..B7. This is the block that you want to change.

4. **Type /SN.**
   Typing /SN selects the Style Numeric Format command and displays the Numeric Format menu.

5. **Type C.**
   Typing C selects Currency from the list of choices. You are prompted to enter the number of decimal places. The default is 2. You can enter any number from 0 to 15.

Easy **Quattro Pro**

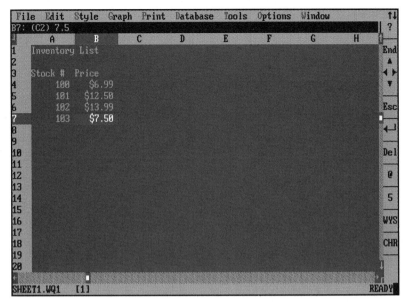

after

Change the column width
If you see asterisks in the column, the entry is too long to fit in the column. To change the column width, see *TASK: Set column width.*

6. Press **Enter**.

   Pressing Enter accepts the default of two decimal places. The cell selector remains in cell B7. The input line displays the entry as you typed it—7.5. The contents in the cell, however, are formatted to show dollar signs and two decimal places—$7.50.

   The input line also displays (C2) before the entry. This indicates the formatting change (currency with two decimal places).

REVIEW

1. Select the block that you want to change.

2. Type **/SNC** to select the Style Numeric Format Currency command.

3. Type the number of decimal places.

4. Press **Enter**.

To display dollar signs

Try a shortcut
You can press the Ctrl-F key combination to select the Style Numeric Format command.

Display commas

before

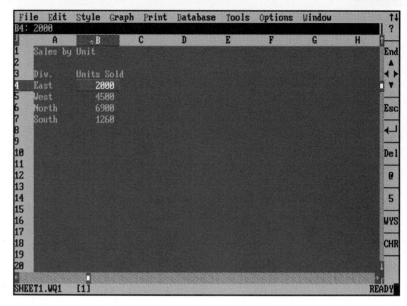

1. **Use the arrow keys to move the cell selector to cell B4.**

   B4 is the first cell in the block that you want to change.

2. **Press Shift-F7.**

   Shift-F7 is the Select key combination. The status indicator displays EXT.

3. **Press the ↓ key three times.**

   Pressing the ↓ key three times highlights the block B4..B7. This is the block that you want to change.

4. **Type /SN.**

   Typing /SN selects the Style Numeric Format command and displays the Numeric Format menu.

5. **Type , (comma).**

   Typing a comma selects the comma format from the list of choices. You are now prompted to enter the number of decimal places. The default is 2. You can enter any number from 0 to 15.

6. **Type 0.**

   Typing 0 tells Quattro Pro that you do not want to display any decimal places.

Easy **Quattro Pro**

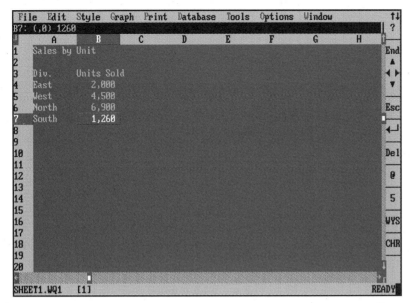

after

Round values
If you select zero decimal places, Quattro Pro rounds the values to fit this format.

7. Press **Enter**.

   Pressing Enter confirms the formatting change. The cell selector remains in cell B7. The input line displays the entry as you typed it (1260). The contents in the cell, however, are formatted to show commas and zero decimal places (1,260).

   The input line also displays (,0) before the entry. This indicates the formatting change (comma with zero decimal places).

REVIEW

1. Select the block that you want to change.

2. Type **/SN,** (comma) to select the Style Numeric Format Comma command.

3. Type the number of decimal places.

4. Press **Enter**.

To display commas

Try a shortcut
You also can press the Ctrl-F key combination to select the Style Numeric Format command.

Display percent signs

Oops!
To undo the formatting change, select the block, type /SN, and select a new format or type R to reset. The Alt-F5 key combination does not undo this change.

before

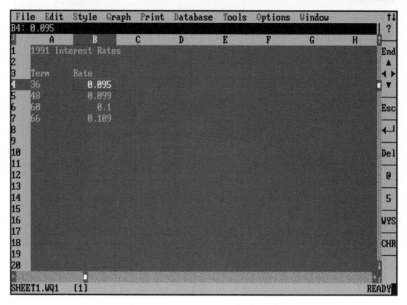

```
 File  Edit  Style  Graph  Print  Database  Tools  Options  Window       ↑↓
B4: 0.095                                                                  ?
      A        B        C        D        E        F        G        H   End
1  1991 Interest Rates                                                     ▲
2                                                                        ◄ ►
3  Term     Rate                                                           ▼
4  36        0.095                                                       Esc
5  48        0.099                                                        ↵
6  60        0.1                                                         Del
7  66        0.109                                                        @
8                                                                         5
9
10                                                                      WYS
11
12                                                                      CHR
13
14
15
16
17
18
19
20
SHEET1.WQ1    [1]                                               READY
```

1. **Use the arrow keys to move the cell selector to cell B4.**

   B4 is the first cell in the block that you want to change.

2. **Press Shift-F7.**

   Shift-F7 is the Select key combination. The status indicator displays EXT.

3. **Press the ↓ key three times.**

   Pressing the ↓ key three times highlights the block B4..B7. This is the block that you want to change. Notice that this cell contains percentages expressed as decimal numbers.

4. **Type /SN.**

   Typing /SN selects the Style Numeric Format command and displays the Numeric Format menu.

5. **Type P.**

   Typing P selects the Percent format from the list of choices. You are prompted to enter the number of decimal places. The default is 2.

6. **Type 1.**

   Typing 1 tells Quattro Pro to display one decimal place.

Easy **Quattro Pro**

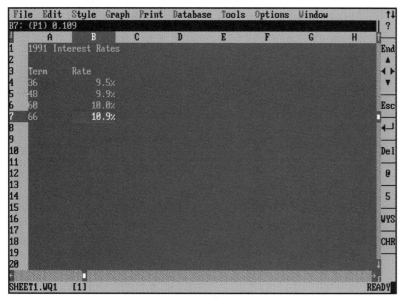

after

Change the column width
If you see asterisks in the column, the entry is too long to fit in the column. To change the column width, see *TASK: Set column width.*

7. Press **Enter**.

   Pressing Enter confirms the formatting change. The cell selector remains in cell B7. The input line displays the entry as you typed it (0.109). The contents in the cell, however, are formatted to show percent signs and one decimal place (10.9%).

   The input line also displays (P1) before the entry. This indicates the formatting change (percentages with one decimal place).

REVIEW

1. Select the block that you want to change.

2. Type **/SNP** to select the Style Numeric Format Percent command.

3. Type the number of decimal places.

4. Press **Enter**.

To display percent signs

Try a shortcut
You also can press the Ctrl-F key combination to select the Style Numeric Format command.

Format a date

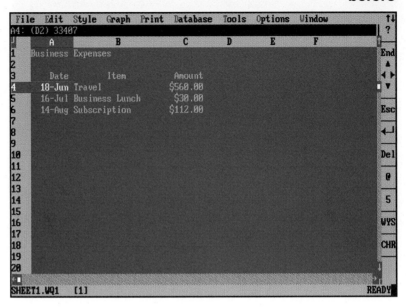

before

```
 File  Edit  Style  Graph  Print  Database  Tools  Options  Window      ↑↓
A4: (D2) 33407                                                            ?
       A            B               C          D        E         F
1   Business Expenses                                                   End
2                                                                        ▲
3       Date         Item          Amount                             ◄ ►
4    18-Jun  Travel              $560.00                              □  ▼
5    16-Jul  Business Lunch       $30.00
6    14-Aug  Subscription        $112.00
7                                                                      Esc
8
9                                                                      ◄┘
10
11                                                                     Del
12
13                                                                      @
14
15                                                                      5
16
17                                                                     WYS
18
19                                                                     CHR
20
SHEET1.WQ1   [1]                                                     READY
```

Oops!
To undo the formatting change, select the block, type /SND, and select a new format. The Alt-F5 key combination does not undo this change.

1. **Use the arrow keys to move the cell selector to cell A4.**

   A4 is the first cell in the block that you want to change. You must use a special method to enter dates. To enter the dates in this example, see *TASK: Enter a date*.

2. **Press Shift-F7.**

   Shift-F7 is the Select key combination. The status indicator displays EXT.

3. **Press the ↓ key twice.**

   Pressing the ↓ key twice highlights the block A4..A6. This is the block that you want to change.

4. **Type /SN.**

   Typing /SN selects the Style Numeric Format command and displays the Numeric Format menu.

5. **Type D.**

   Typing D selects Date from the menu and displays a list of date formats.

6. **Type 4.**

   Typing 4 selects the long international format. The default for this format is *06/18/91*. (You can change the international format. See the Quattro Pro manual or *Using Quattro Pro 3,* Special Edition for more information.)

   The cell selector remains in cell A6. The input line still displays the

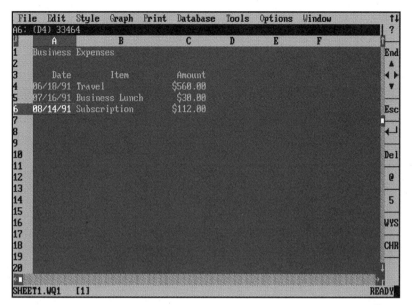

after

serial number for the date. But the cell displays the date in the
format `08/14/91`. `(D4)` appears on the input line, which indicates
the format change.

1. Select the block that you want to change.

2. Type **/SND** to select the Style Numeric Format Date
   command.

3. Select the date format that you want:

Format	Example
Format	*Example*
1 DD-MMM-YY	14-Aug-91
2 DD-MMM	14-Aug (current year)
3 MMM-YY	Aug-91
4 MM/DD/YY	08/14/91
5 MM/DD	08/14 (current year)

**Change the column
width**
If you see asterisks in the
column, the entry is too
long to fit in the column.
To change the column
width, see *TASK: Set
column width*.

**To format
a date**

Try a shortcut
You also can press the
Ctrl-F key combination to
select the Style Numeric
Format command.

Formatting the Spreadsheet

Format a time

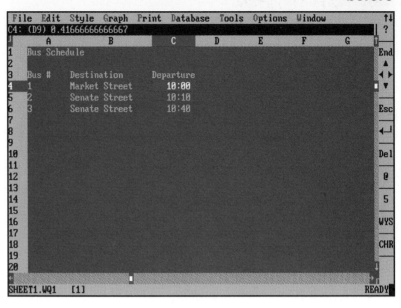

1. **Use the arrow keys to move the cell selector to cell C4.**

   C4 is the first cell in the block that you want to change. Remember that to enter times, you must use a special method. To enter the times in this example, see *TASK: Enter a time*.

2. **Press Shift-F7.**

   Shift-F7 is the Select key combination. The status indicator displays EXT.

3. **Press the ↓ key twice.**

   Pressing the ↓ key twice highlights the block B4..B6. This is the block that you want to change.

4. **Type /SN.**

   Typing /SN selects the Style Numeric Format command and displays the Numeric Format menu.

5. **Type D.**

   Typing D selects Date from the menu and displays a list of date formats.

6. **Type T.**

   Typing T displays the available time formats.

Easy **Quattro Pro**

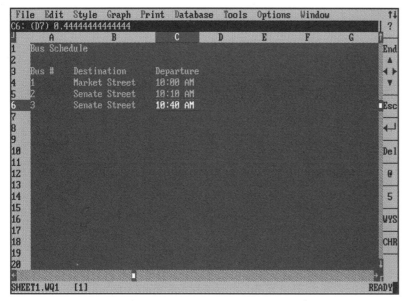

after

Change the column width
If you see asterisks in the column, the entry is too large to fit in the column. To change the column width, see *TASK: Set column width*.

7. Type **2**.

Typing 2 selects the HH:MM AM format, which displays times as *10:40 AM*. The entries in the block are formatted with this style. On the input line, you see the serial number for that time. (D7) also appears on the input line, which indicates the time format.

To format a time

1. Select the block that you want to change.

2. Type **/SNDT** to select the Style Numeric Format Date Time command.

3. Select the time format that you want:

Format	Example
1 HH:MM:SS AM/PM	10:00:30 AM
2 HH:MM AM/PM	10:00 AM
3 HH:MM:SS	13:00:30
4 HH:MM	13:00

Try a shortcut
You can press the Ctrl-F key combination to select the Style Numeric Format command.

Insert a row

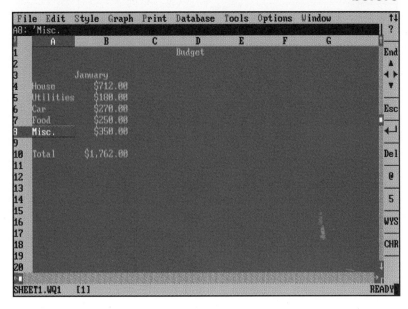

before

```
File Edit Style Graph Print Database Tools Options Window    ↑↓
A8: 'Misc.                                                    ?
      A         B         C      D       E       F       G
1                              Budget                       End
2                                                            ▲
3          January                                          ◄ ►
4     House      $712.00                                     ▼
5     Utilities  $100.00
6     Car        $270.00                                    Esc
7     Food       $250.00
8     Misc.      $350.00                                     ◄┘
9
10    Total    $1,762.00                                    Del
11                                                           @
12
13                                                           5
14
15                                                          WYS
16
17                                                          CHR
18
19
20
SHEET1.WQ1   [1]                                          READY
```

Oops!
To undo the row insertion, press the Alt-F5 key combination immediately after inserting the row.

1. **Use the arrow keys to move the cell selector to cell A8.**
   The new row will be inserted above row 8. You can position the cell selector in any column in the row.

2. **Type /EI.**
   Typing /EI selects the Edit Insert command and displays two choices: Rows and Columns.

3. **Type R.**
   Typing R selects Rows. You see the prompt Enter row insert block: A8..A8. A8 is the current cell.

4. **Press Enter.**
   Pressing Enter inserts one row above row 8.

Easy **Quattro Pro**

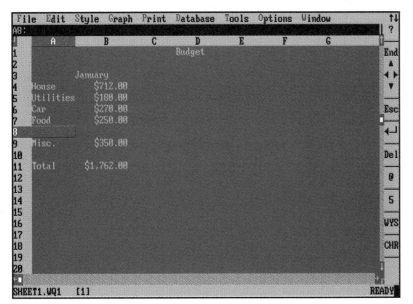

after

Format the new row
Cell formats are not
copied to the new row
automatically. You need
to format all the columns
in the row.

REVIEW

1. Move the cell selector to where you want to insert the row.

2. Type **/EIR** to select the Edit Insert Rows command.

3. Type the block address of the row(s) that you want to insert. Or use the arrow keys to select the number of rows that you want to insert.

4. Press **Enter**.

To insert a row

Try a shortcut
You can also press the
Ctrl-I key combination to
select the Edit Insert
command.

Formatting the Spreadsheet

Delete a row

before

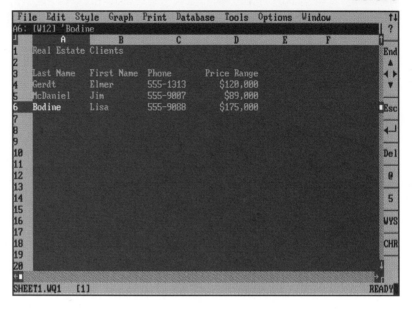

```
 File  Edit  Style  Graph  Print  Database  Tools  Options  Window    ↑↓
A6: [W12] 'Bodine                                                      ?
      A          B          C          D          E          F         U
1  Real Estate Clients                                                End
2                                                                      ▲
3  Last Name  First Name Phone       Price Range                     ◄ ►
4  Gerdt      Elmer      555-1313       $120,000                       ▼
5  McDaniel   Jim        555-9087        $89,000
6  Bodine     Lisa       555-9088       $175,000                     ■Esc
7                                                                      ↵
8
9                                                                     Del
10
11                                                                     @
12
13                                                                     5
14
15                                                                    WYS
16
17                                                                    CHR
18
19
20
SHEET1.WQ1    [1]                                                   READY
```

Oops!
To restore a deleted row,
press the Alt-F5 key
combination immediately
after the deletion.

1. **Use the arrow keys to move the cell selector to cell A6.**
   Row 6 is the row that you want to delete. You can position the cell selector in any column in the row.

2. **Type /ED.**
   Typing /ED selects the Edit Delete command and displays two choices: Rows and Columns.

3. **Type R.**
   Typing R selects Rows. You see the prompt `Enter block of rows to delete: A6..A6`. A6 is the current cell.

4. **Press Enter.**
   Pressing Enter deletes the current row.

Easy **Quattro Pro**

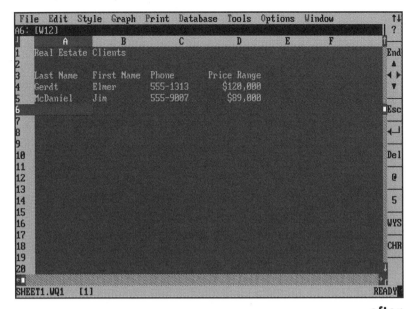

after

Be careful!
When you delete a row, you delete all the data in that row—including any data that is off-screen. Be sure to check the entire row before you delete it.

To delete a row

1. Move the cell selector to the row that you want to delete.

2. Type **/EDR** to select the Edit Delete Rows command.

3. Use the arrow keys to highlight the row(s) that you want to delete. Or type the block address of the row(s) that you want to delete.

4. Press **Enter**.

Insert a column

before

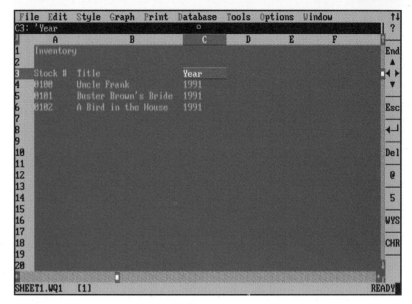

1. **Use the arrow keys to move the cell selector to cell C3.**
   The new column will be inserted to the left of this column. You can position the cell selector in any row in the column.

2. **Type /EI.**
   Typing /EI selects the Edit Insert command and displays two choices: Rows and Columns.

3. **Type C.**
   Typing C selects Columns. You see the prompt `Enter column insert block: C3..C3`. C3 is the current cell.

4. **Press Enter.**
   Pressing Enter inserts one column.

Easy **Quattro Pro**

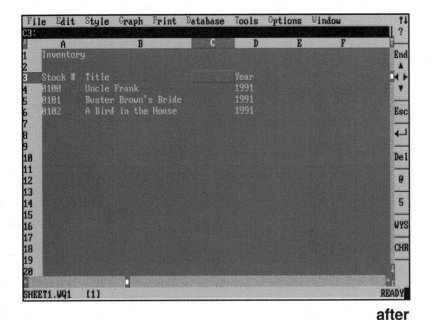

after

Try a shortcut
You can press the Ctrl-I key combination to select the Edit Insert command.

1. Move the cell selector to the right of where you want the new column.

2. Type **/EIC** to select the Edit Insert Columns command.

3. Use the arrow keys to select the number of columns that you want to insert. Or type the cell coordinates of the column(s) that you want to insert.

4. Press **Enter**.

To insert a column

Delete a column

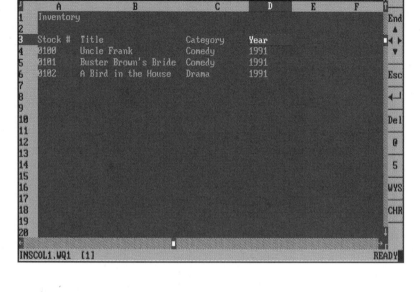

Oops!
To restore a deleted column, press the Alt-F5 key combination immediately after deleting the column.

1. **Use the arrow keys to move the cell selector to cell D3.**
    Column D is the column that you want to delete. You can position the cell selector in any row in the column.

2. **Type /ED.**
    Typing /ED selects the Edit Delete command and displays two choices: Rows and Columns.

3. **Type C.**
    Typing C selects Columns. You see the prompt `Delete one or more columns: D3`. D3 is the current cell.

4. **Press Enter.**
    Pressing Enter deletes the current column.

Easy Quattro Pro

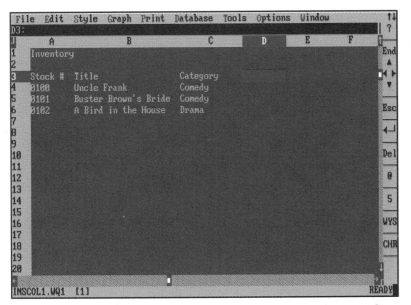

after

Be careful!
When you delete a column, Quattro Pro deletes all the data in that column, even data that is off-screen. Make sure that you don't accidentally delete data that you need.

1. Move the cell selector to the column that you want to delete.

2. Type **/EDC** to select the Edit Delete Columns command.

3. Use the arrow keys to highlight the number of columns that you want to delete. Or type the block address of the column(s) that you want to delete.

4. Press **Enter**.

To delete a column

Hide columns

before

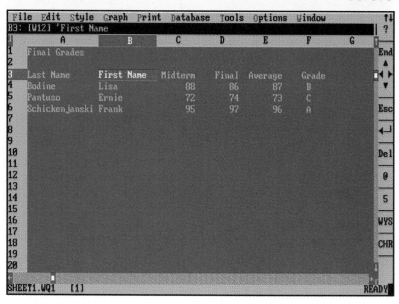

```
File  Edit  Style  Graph  Print  Database  Tools  Options  Window          ↑↓
B3: [W12] 'First Name                                                        ?
          A              B          C        D        E        F        G
1    Final Grades                                                          End
2                                                                           ▲
3    Last Name      First Name   Midterm   Final   Average   Grade        ◄ ►
4    Bodine         Lisa           88        86       87        B           ▼
5    Pantuso        Ernie          72        74       73        C
6    Schickenjanski Frank          95        97       96        A          Esc
7                                                                           ↵
8
9                                                                          Del
10
11                                                                          @
12
13                                                                          5
14
15
16                                                                         WYS
17
18                                                                         CHR
19
20
SHEET1.WQ1    [1]                                                       READY
```

Oops!
To redisplay the columns,
type /SHE, type the block
address of the columns,
and press Enter.

1. **Use the arrow keys to move the cell selector to cell B3.**

   Column B is the first column that you want to hide. You can place the cell selector in any row in the column.

2. **Type /SH.**

   Typing /SH selects the Style Hide Column command and displays two choices: Hide and Expose.

3. **Type H.**

   Typing H selects Hide. You see the prompt Hide columns from view: B3. B3 is the current cell.

4. **Type B3..E3.**

   B3..E3 is the block of columns that you want to hide.

5. **Press Enter.**

   Pressing Enter hides the columns on-screen. The information is still intact in the spreadsheet; you just cannot see it. You can see by the column numbering (A, F, G) that columns B–E are hidden.

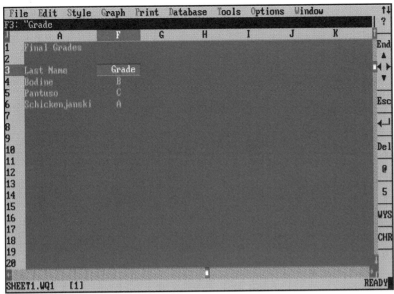

after

What about Undo?
You cannot use Undo to
redisplay hidden columns.

1. Move the cell pointer to the first column that you want to hide.

2. Type **/SHH** to select the Style Hide Column Hide command.

3. Type the block coordinates of the column(s) that you want to hide.

4. Press **Enter**.

To hide columns

Advanced Editing

This section covers the following tasks:

Total cells with the @SUM function

Copy a formula

Calculate an average

Copy a block

Erase a block

Move a block

Fill a block

Protect the spreadsheet

Name a block

List block names

Sort data

Replace data

Total cells with the @SUM function

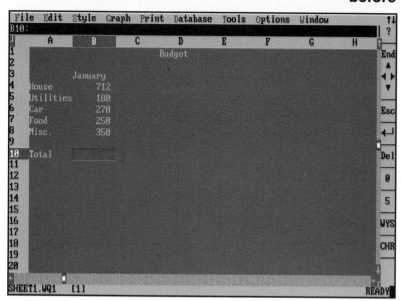

1. **Use the arrow keys to move the cell selector to cell B10.**

   Cell B10 will display the result of the @SUM function.

2. **Type @SUM(.**

   @SUM is the name of a function that automatically sums entries in a block. You enter the block that you want to sum within the parentheses.

3. **Press the ↑ key six times.**

   When you press the ↑ key, the mode indicator displays POINT, which reminds you that you can point to the cells that you want to include.

   Pressing the ↑ key six times moves the cell selector to B4. This is the first cell in the block that you want to sum. You see @SUM(B4 on the input line.

4. **Press Shift-F7.**

   Shift-F7 is the Select key combination. You use this key combination to select the block that you want. The input line changes to @SUM(B4..B4.

5. **Press the ↓ key four times.**

   Pressing the ↓ key four times includes the block B4..B8 in the formula. The input line displays @SUM(B4..B8.

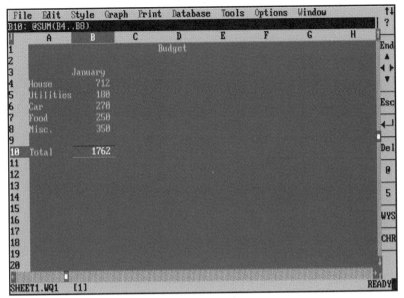

after

Why use the @SUM function?
The @SUM function enables you to sum a block. If you later insert or delete rows or columns within the block, the total is updated automatically.

Select a block with the mouse
To select a block with the mouse, click on the first cell that you want to include. Press and hold the mouse button and drag the mouse across the block. Release the mouse button.

6. Type).

Typing) tells Quattro Pro that you are finished selecting the block. The block is inserted into the parentheses. On the input line, you see @SUM(B4..B8).

7. Press **Enter**.

You see the result of the function in the cell—1762. The input line displays the function—@SUM(B4..B8).

REVIEW

To total cells with the @SUM function

1. Move the cell selector to the cell where you want the sum to appear.

2. Type @SUM(.

3. Select the block that you want to sum by typing the block address, using the arrow keys, or using the mouse.

4. Type).

5. Press **Enter**.

Copy a formula

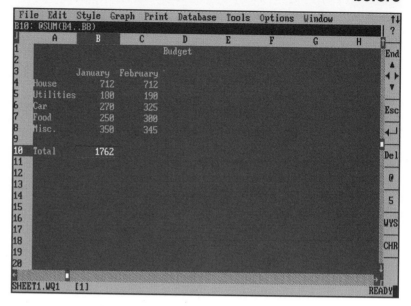

Oops!
To undo a copy, press the Alt-F5 key combination immediately after making the copy.

1. **Use the arrow keys to move the cell selector to cell B10.**

   You see B10: on the input line, followed by the cell contents. This is the formula that you want to copy. (To create the formula, see *TASK: Total cells with the @SUM function.*)

2. **Type /EC.**

   Typing /EC selects the Edit Copy command. You see the prompt Source block of cells: B10..B10. B10 is the current cell, and it contains the formula that you want to copy. Quattro Pro is now in POINT mode.

3. **Press Enter.**

   Pressing Enter confirms that you want to copy this cell.

   You see the prompt Destination for cells: B10. B10 is the current cell.

4. **Press the → key once.**

   Pressing the → key once moves the cell selector to cell C10. This is the cell where you want the copy to appear.

5. **Press Enter.**

   The result of the formula appears in cell C10, and the cell selector returns to cell B10.

Easy **Quattro Pro**

```
 File  Edit  Style  Graph  Print  Database  Tools  Options  Window    ↑↓
C10: @SUM(C4..C8)                                                        ?
    A        B        C        D        E        F        G        H
 1                          Budget                                      End
 2                                                                      ▲
 3           January  February                                         ◄ ►
 4  House      712      712                                            ▼
 5  Utilities  180      190
 6  Car        270      325                                            Esc
 7  Food       250      300
 8  Misc.      350      345                                            ↵
 9
10  Total     1762     1872                                            Del
11                                                                      @
12
13                                                                      5
14
15                                                                     WYS
16
17                                                                     CHR
18
19
20                                                                      ↓
SHEET1.WQ1   [1]                                                     READY
```

after

6. Press the → key **once**.

Pressing the → key once returns the cell pointer to cell C10. Notice
that the input line contains the formula @SUM(C4..C8). This
formula references the current column.

The formula changes because of a Quattro Pro concept known
as *relative addressing*. Quattro Pro adjusts cell references
automatically when you copy a formula. For more information on
relative addresses, see the Quattro Pro manual or *Using Quattro
Pro 3*, Special Edition.

1. Move the cell selector to the cell containing the formula
   that you want to copy.

2. Type **/EC** to select the Edit Copy command.

3. Press **Enter** to specify the current cell as the source. Or
   type a new source cell.

4. Type or point to the destination cell (or block of cells).

5. Press **Enter**.

**Copy a formula to a
block**
You also can copy one
formula to an entire block.
Follow this same
procedure, but point to or
type a block for the
destination.

To copy a formula

Try a shortcut
You also can press the
Ctrl-C key combination to
select the Edit Copy
command.

Calculate an average

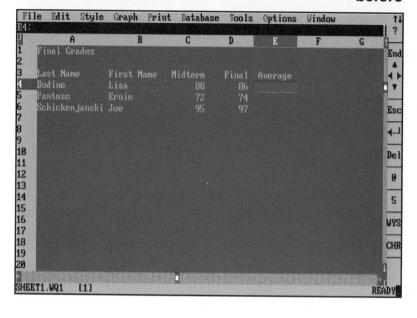

before

1. **Use the arrow keys to move the cell selector to cell E4.**

   Cell E4 will display the result of the @AVG formula.

2. **Type @AVG(.**

   @AVG is the name of the function that automatically averages entries in a block. You enter the block that you want to average within the parentheses.

3. **Press the ← key twice.**

   When you press the ← key, the mode indicator displays POINT. This reminds you that you can point to the block.

   Pressing the ← key once moves the cell selector to C4. This is the first cell in the block that you want to average. On the input line, you see @AVG(C4.

4. **Press Shift-F7.**

   Shift-F7 is the Select key combination. You use this key combination to select the block that you want. The input line displays @AVG(C4..

5. **Press the → key once.**

   Pressing the → key once includes the block C4..D4 in the formula. The input line displays @AVG(C4..D4.

Easy **Quattro Pro**

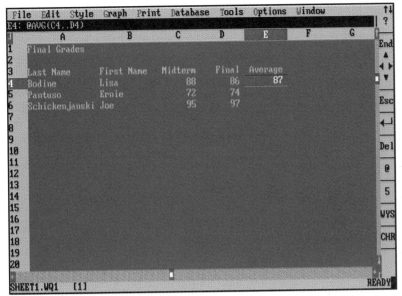

after

6. Type).

Typing a right parenthesis tells Quattro Pro that you are finished selecting the block. The block is inserted into the parentheses. The input line displays `@AVG(C4..D4)`.

7. **Press Enter.**

You see the result of the function in the cell—`87`. The input line displays the function—`@AVG(C4..D4)`. You can finish the spreadsheet by copying E4 to the block E5..E6. (See *TASK: Copy a block*.)

Select a block with the mouse
To point to a block with the mouse, click on the first cell that you want to include. Press and hold the mouse button and drag the mouse across the block. Release the mouse button.

REVIEW

1. Move the cell selector to the cell where you want the average to appear.

2. Type **@AVG(**.

3. Select the block that you want to average by pointing to it with the arrow keys or the mouse.

4. Type **)**.

5. Press **Enter**.

To calculate an average

Use other functions
Quattro Pro offers over 114 useful, timesaving functions. See the Quattro Pro manual or *Using Quattro Pro 3, Special Edition*.

Advanced Editing

137

Copy a block

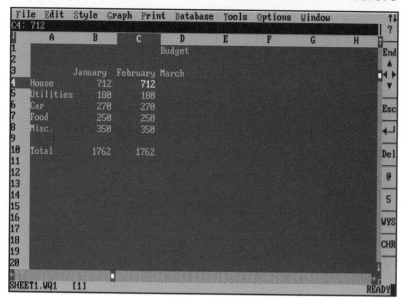

Oops!
To delete the copy, press the Alt-F5 key combination immediately after making the copy.

1. **Use the arrow keys to move the cell selector to cell C4.**

   C4 is the first cell in the block that you want to copy.

2. **Press Shift-F7.**

   Shift-F7 is the Select key combination. You use this key combination to select the block that you want. The status indicator displays EXT.

3. **Press the ↓ key six times.**

   Pressing the ↓ key six times selects the block C4..C10. This is the block that you want to copy.

4. **Type /EC.**

   Typing /EC selects the Edit Copy command. Because you have already selected the block, you are not prompted for the source cells. You see the prompt Destination for cells: C10. C10 is the current cell.

138

Easy **Quattro Pro**

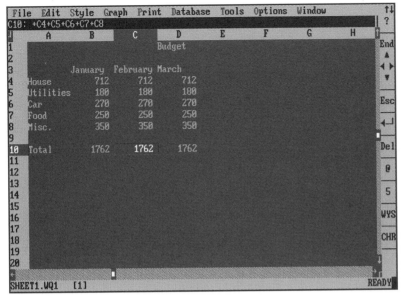

```
 File  Edit  Style  Graph  Print  Database  Tools  Options  Window    ↑↓
C10:  +C4+C5+C6+C7+C8                                                   ?
      A         B         C         D        E       F       G      H
1                              Budget                                  End
2                                                                       ▲
3               January  February  March                              ◄ ►
4  House          712       712      712                                ▼
5  Utilities      180       180      180
6  Car            270       270      270                               Esc
7  Food           250       250      250
8  Misc.          350       350      350                               ↵
9
10 Total         1762      1762     1762                               Del
11                                                                      @
12
13                                                                      5
14
15                                                                     WYS
16
17                                                                     CHR
18
19
20
SHEET1.WQ1    [1]                                                    READY
```

after

5. Type **D4**.

   D4 is the first cell of the area where you want to place the copied block. The copied block takes the same shape and space as the original. Be careful not to overwrite existing data.

6. Press **Enter**.

   The block is copied to the new location. The cell selector returns to cell C10.

Select a block with the mouse

To point to a block with the mouse, click on the first cell that you want to include. Press and hold the mouse button and drag the mouse across the block. Release the mouse button.

REVIEW

To copy a block

1. Select the block that you want to copy.

2. Type **/EC** to select the Edit Copy command.

3. Type or point to the destination.

4. Press **Enter**.

Try a shortcut

You can press the Ctrl-C key combination to select the Edit Copy command.

Advanced Editing

139

Erase a block

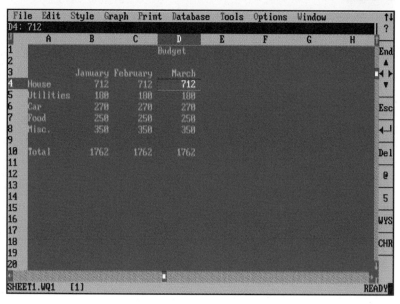

Oops!
To restore an erased block, press the Alt-F5 key combination immediately after erasing the block.

1. **Use the arrow keys to move the cell selector to cell D4.**

   D4 is the first cell in the block that you want to erase.

2. **Press Shift-F7.**

   Shift-F7 is the Select key combination. You use this key combination to select the block that you want. The status indicator displays EXT.

3. **Press the ↓ key four times.**

   Pressing the ↓ key four times selects the block D4..D8. This is the block that you want to erase.

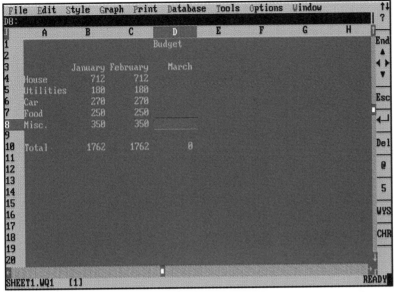

after

4. Press the **Del** key.

   Pressing the Del key erases the block. The column total in cell D10 is adjusted.

1. Select the block that you want to erase.

2. Press the **Del** key.

To erase a block

Be careful!
When you erase a block that is included in a formula, the formula is recalculated. Be sure that you don't erase any values that you need for the formula to be correct.

Use a different method
You also can use the Edit Erase command to erase a block. Select the block, type /EE, and press Enter.

Move a block

Oops!
To restore a moved block to its original position, press the Alt-F5 key combination immediately after you move the block.

before

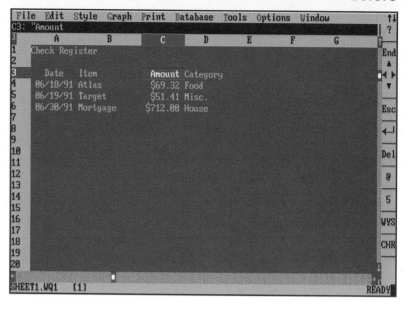

```
File  Edit  Style  Graph  Print  Database  Tools  Options  Window      ↑↓
C3: "Amount                                                              ?
        A         B         C         D         E         F      G
1 Check Register                                                       End
2                                                                       ▲
3     Date    Item        Amount Category                            ◄┤ ►
4  06/18/91 Atlas        $69.32 Food                                    ▼
5  06/19/91 Target       $51.41 Misc.
6  06/30/91 Mortgage    $712.00 House                                  Esc
7                                                                       ◄┘
8
9
10                                                                     Del
11                                                                      @
12
13                                                                      5
14
15
16                                                                    WYS
17
18                                                                    CHR
19
20
G
SHEET1.WQ1    [1]                                               READY
```

1. **Use the arrow keys to move the cell selector to cell C3.**

   C3 is the first cell in the block that you want to move.

2. **Press Shift-F7.**

   Shift-F7 is the Select key combination. You use this key combination to select the block that you want. The status indicator displays EXT.

3. **Press the ↓ key three times.**

   Pressing the ↓ key three times selects the block C3..C6. This is the block that you want to move.

4. **Type /EM.**

   Typing /EM selects the Edit Move command. Because you have already selected the block, you are not prompted for the source cells. You see the prompt Destination for cells: C6. C6 is the current cell.

5. **Type E3.**

   E3 is the first cell of the area where you want to insert the block. The block is the same shape and size of the original. Be careful not to overwrite existing data.

Easy **Quattro Pro**

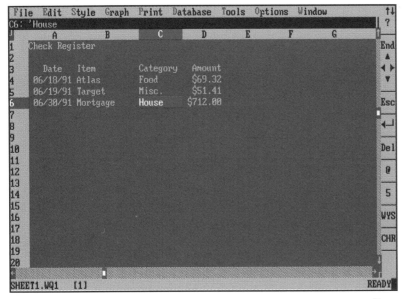

after

6. Press **Enter**.

   The block is moved to the new location. The cell selector returns to cell C6. You can use this process to rearrange the spreadsheet.

   Next delete column C, which is now empty.

7. Type **/EDC**.

   Typing /EDC selects the Edit Delete Columns command.

8. Press **Enter**.

   Pressing Enter confirms the command, and the column is deleted.

1. Select the block that you want to move.

2. Type **/EM** to select the Edit Move command.

3. Type or point to the destination.

4. Press **Enter**.

To move a block

Try a shortcut
You also can press the Ctrl-M key combination to select the Edit Move command.

Fill a block

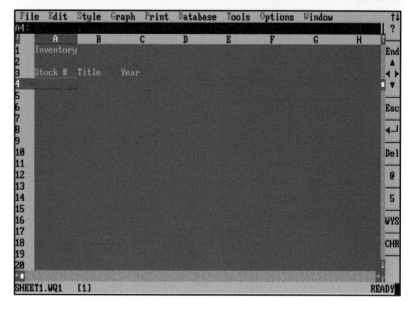

before

Oops!
To undo the fill, press the Alt-F5 key combination immediately after entering the fill.

1. **Use the arrow keys to place the cell selector in cell A4.**
   A4 is the first cell that you want to fill.

2. **Press Shift-F7.**
   Shift-F7 is the Select key combination. The status indicator displays EXT.

3. **Press the ↓ key three times.**
   Pressing the ↓ key three times selects block A4..A7. This is the block that you want to fill.

4. **Type /EF.**
   Typing /EF selects the Edit Fill command. You are prompted to specify the start value.

5. **Type 100.**
   100 is the number with which you want to start.

6. **Press Enter.**
   Pressing Enter confirms the starting number. You are prompted for the Step value. The default is 1.

7. **Press Enter.**
   Pressing Enter accepts the default step value. You are prompted for a stop value. The default, 8191, is displayed.

Easy **Quattro Pro**

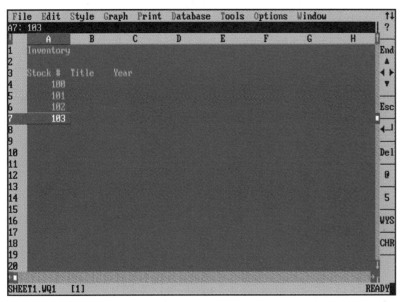

after

8. Press **Enter**.

Because you have already specified the block, you do not need to specify the stop value. Quattro Pro fills only the selected block.

On-screen, the block that you selected is filled with numbers, starting with 100 and added in increments of one.

1. Select the block that you want to fill.

2. Type **/EF** to select the Edit Fill command.

3. Press **Enter** to accept the preselected block.

4. Type a Start value and press **Enter**.

5. Type a Step value and press **Enter**.

6. Type a Stop value and press **Enter**.

Select a block with the mouse

To select a block with the mouse, click on the first cell that you want to include. Press and hold the mouse button and drag the mouse across the block. Release the mouse button.

To fill a block

Protect the spreadsheet

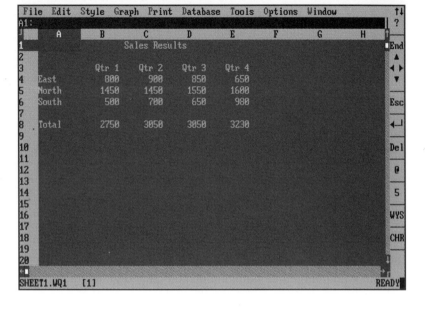

Oops!
To turn off protection for a spreadsheet, type /OPD.

1. **Type /OP.**

   Typing /OP selects the Option Protection command. On-screen you see a menu with two choices: Enable and Disable.

2. **Type E.**

   Typing E selects Enable and turns on spreadsheet protection. You must turn on Enable to protect the cells from changes.

3. **Type Q.**

   Typing Q selects Quit and closes the menu.

   You cannot make any changes or delete any of the entries in the spreadsheet.

   You will now test the protection to make sure that it is turned on.

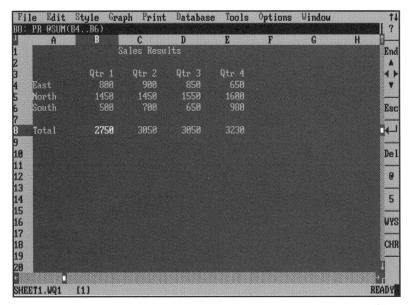

File Edit Style Graph Print Database Tools Options Window   ↑↓
B8: PR @SUM(B4..B6)   ?
     A   B   C   D   E   F   G   H End
1   Sales Results   ▲
2   ◄ ►
3   Qtr 1   Qtr 2   Qtr 3   Qtr 4   ▼
4 East   800   900   850   650
5 North   1450   1450   1550   1600
6 South   500   700   650   980   Esc
7
8 Total   2750   3050   3050   3230   ↵
9
10   Del
11
12   @
13
14   5
15
16   WYS
17
18   CHR
19
20
SHEET1.WQ1   [1]   READY

after

4. Move the cell selector to cell B8, type **1**, and press
   Enter.

   You see the error message Error Protected cell or block.
   Notice that the input line displays PR, which indicates that the cell
   is protected.

5. Press **Esc**.

   Pressing the Esc key clears the error message.

Type **/OPE** to select the Options Protection Enable
command.

Unprotect a block
To undo the protection for
a selected block, select
the block and then type
/SPU to select the Style
Protection Unprotect
command.

REVIEW

To
protect the
spreadsheet

Name a block

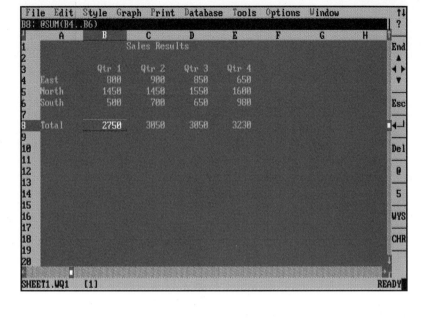

Oops!
To delete a block name,
type /END, highlight the
name, and press Enter.

1. **Use the arrow keys to move the cell selector to cell B8.**
   This is the cell that you want to name.

2. **Type /EN.**
   Typing /EN selects the Edit Names command. A menu appears.

3. **Type C.**
   Typing C selects Create from the list. You see the prompt `Enter name to create/modify:`.

4. **Type QTR1.**
   QTR1 is the name that you want to assign this block; in this case, the block is a single cell. The block name can be up to 15 characters long. As a general rule, use only alphanumeric characters and don't use a name that looks like a cell address (such as *B15*).

5. **Press Enter.**
   You see the prompt `Enter block: B8..B8`. B8 is the current cell; this is the cell that you want to name.

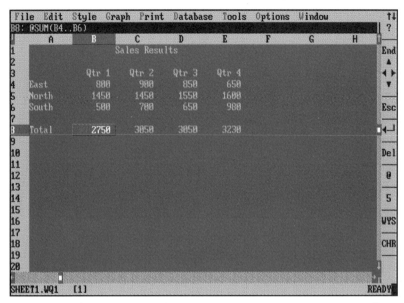

after

6. Press **Enter**.

    Pressing Enter confirms the block to name. Nothing changes
    on-screen. The cell and the input line look the same as before.
    (The Before and After screens are identical.) The name is saved
    with the spreadsheet when you save the spreadsheet.

1. Select the block that you want to name.

2. Type **/ENC** to select the Edit Names Create command.

3. Type the block name.

4. Press **Enter**.

What is a block?
A block is any rectangular area of cells. A block can be any size—including just one cell.

To name a block

Why use block names?
Names are easy to remember; you can use the names in formulas; and you can use the F5 (GoTo) key to move to a named block quickly.

List block names

```
 File  Edit  Style  Graph  Print  Database  Tools  Options  Window        ↑↓
A10:                                                                        ?
     A       B       C       D       E       F       G       H
 1                  Sales Results                                         End
 2                                                                         ▲
 3           Qtr 1   Qtr 2   Qtr 3   Qtr 4                               ◄ ►
 4  East      800     900     850     650                                  ▼
 5  North    1450    1450    1550    1600
 6  South     500     700     650     980                                 Esc
 7
 8  Total    2750    3050    3050    3230                                 ↵
 9
10                                                                       Del
11
12                                                                         @
13
14                                                                         5
15
16                                                                       WYS
17
18                                                                       CHR
19
20
SHEET1.WQ1    [1]                                                       READY
```

Oops!
To delete the list,
press the Alt-F5 key
combination immediately
after creating it.

1. **Create the names that you want to use.**
    To list names, you first must create them. To create a name, see
    TASK: Name a block.

2. **Use the arrow keys to move the cell selector to cell A10.**
    A10 is the first cell of the area where you want the list of names to
    appear. The list of names is two columns wide and as many rows
    deep as there are names. Be sure that you do not insert the table
    where you might overwrite any data.

3. **Type /EN.**
    Typing /EN selects the Edit Names command. A menu appears.

4. **Type M.**
    Typing M selects the Make Table command. You see the prompt
    Enter block A10..A10. A10 is the current cell.

5. **Press Enter.**
    Pressing Enter inserts the beginning of the table in cell A10.
    On-screen, you see a two-column list. The first column lists the
    block names; the second column lists the coordinates for the
    block. This example shows four names. If you have not created that
    many names, you will see only the names that you have created.

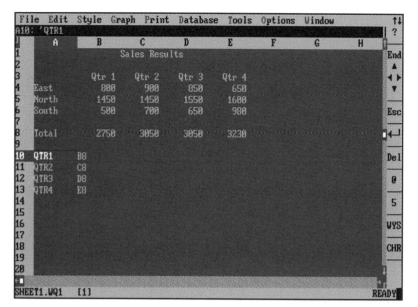

```
 File  Edit  Style  Graph  Print  Database  Tools  Options  Window    ↑↓
A10:  'QTR1                                                           │  ?
│        A        B        C        D        E        F        G     H │┌─┐
1│                   Sales Results                                    │End
2│                                                                    │ ▲
3│              Qtr 1    Qtr 2    Qtr 3    Qtr 4                       │◄ ►
4│  East          800      900      850      650                      │ ▼
5│  North        1450     1450     1550     1600                      │
6│  South         500      700      650      980                      │Esc
7│                                                                    │
8│  Total        2750     3050     3050     3230                      │■◄┘
9│                                                                    │
10│ QTR1    B8                                                         │Del
11│ QTR2    C8                                                         │
12│ QTR3    D8                                                         │ @
13│ QTR4    E8                                                         │
14│                                                                    │ 5
15│                                                                    │
16│                                                                    │WYS
17│                                                                    │
18│                                                                    │CHR
19│                                                                    │
20│                                                                    │
└■                                                                    ■│
SHEET1.WQ1    [1]                                              READY
```

after

1. Move the cell selector to the first cell in the block that will contain the list.

2. Type **/ENM** to select the Edit Names Make Table command.

3. Press **Enter** to insert the table, starting in the current cell. Or type the coordinates of the location where you want to insert the table.

Create names
If you see nothing on-screen, you may not have created any names. You must create names before you can list them.

REVIEW

To list block names

Delete the list
If you later want to delete the list of block names, select the block and press the Del key.

Sort data

(Part 1 of 2)

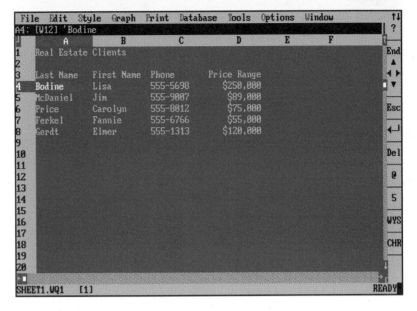

Oops!
If you select the wrong block, type /DSR to select the Database Sort Reset command. Then start over.

Sorting data is a two-part process. The first part, Select the block, is covered on these two pages. Turn the page for the second part, Perform the sort.

1. **Use the arrow keys to move the cell selector to cell A4.**

   A4 is the first cell in the block that you want to sort.

2. **Press Shift-F7.**

   Shift-F7 is the Select key combination. You use this key combination to select the block that you want. The status indicator displays EXT.

3. **Press the ↓ key four times.**

   Pressing the ↓ key four times highlights the block A4..A8. This is the block that you want to sort.

4. **Press the → key three times.**

   Pressing the → key three times extends the block to include A4..D8. If other data in the row is connected to that column (for example, the address list), you must be sure to include the entire block—not only the column that you want to sort. If you select only the column, the entries become mismatched.

   Be sure to select only the data—not any row or column headings.

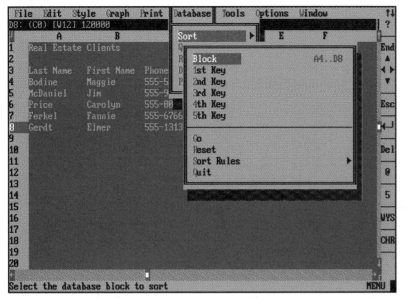

after

5. Type **/DS**.

   Typing /DS selects the Database Sort command. A menu appears.

6. Type **B**.

   Typing B tells Quattro Pro to use the block that you just selected.
   Make sure this block includes all columns and rows. A4..D8
   appears next to the Block menu option.

Select a block with the mouse

To select a block with the mouse, click on the first cell that you want to include. Press and hold the mouse button and drag the mouse across the block. Release the mouse button.

1. Select the block that you want to sort.

2. Type **/DS** to select the Database Sort command.

3. Type **B** to select Block.

To sort data

(Part 1 of 2)

Sort data

(Part 2 of 2)

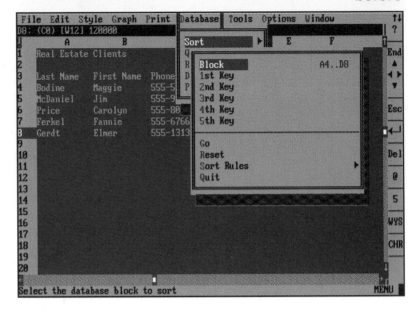

Oops!
To restore the block to its original order, press the Alt-F5 key combination immediately after sorting it.

Sorting data is a two-part process. The first part, Select the block, is covered on the preceding two pages. These two pages cover the second part, Perform the sort.

1. **Type 1.**

   Typing 1 selects 1st Key and tells Quattro Pro that you want to sort on the first key of entries in the block. You see the prompt Column to be used as first sort key: D8.

2. **Type A4.**

   Typing A4 tells Quattro Pro to sort the entries in column A, which is the first column. You can select any row in this column.

3. **Press Enter.**

   Pressing Enter verifies this sort key. You see a dialog box that asks you for the sort order (A or D).

4. **Type A.**

   Typing A selects ascending order.

5. **Press Enter.**

   Pressing Enter confirms the sort order. A menu appears. On the menu, you see the block to sort, the first sort key, and the sorting order. For this example, you see A4..A4 A. This indicates that A4 is the sort key and A or ascending is the sort order.

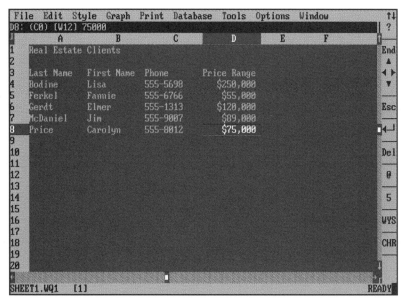

after

6. Type **G**.

   Typing G selects Go from the menu. The data is sorted on-screen in alphabetical order by last name.

Sort numbers
You can use this same procedure to sort numbers.

REVIEW

1. Type **1** to select 1st Sort key.

2. Type or point to the column to use as the sort key.

3. Press **Enter**.

4. Type **A** or **D** to specify ascending or descending order.

5. Type **G** to select Go.

Sort data

(Part 2 of 2)

Sort on more than one key
You can sort on more than one key. For complete sort information, see *Using Quattro Pro 3,* Special Edition.

Replace data

(Part 1 of 2)

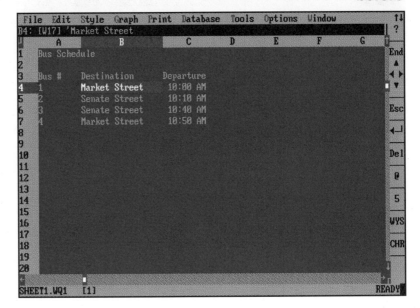

Oops!
If you select the wrong block, press Esc and then start over.

Replacing data is a two-part process. The first part, Specify the search block, is covered on these two pages. Turn the page for the second part, Make the replacements.

1. **Use the arrow keys to move the cell selector to cell B4.**

   B4 is the first cell in the block that you want to search for data to replace.

2. **Press Shift-F7.**

   Shift-F7 is the Select key combination. You use this key combination to select the block that you want. The status indicator displays EXT.

3. **Press the ↓ key three times.**

   Pressing the ↓ key three times selects the block B4..B7. This is the block that you want to search.

Easy **Quattro Pr**

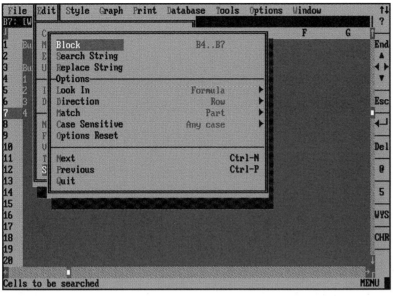

4. Type **/ES**.

Typing /ES selects the Edit Search & Replace command. A menu appears on-screen.

5. Type **B**.

Typing B tells Quattro Pro to use the block. The block address appears on the menu. For this example, you see B4..B7.

REVIEW

1. Select the block to search.

2. Type **/ES** to select the Edit Search & Replace command.

3. Type **B** to select Block.

To replace data
(Part 1 of 2)

Replace data

(Part 2 of 2)

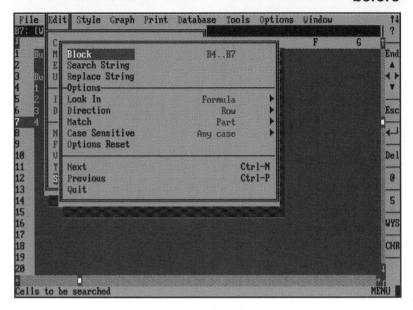

Oops!
You can undo the last replacement with the Alt-F5 key combination.

Replacing data is a two-part process. The first part, Specify the search block, is covered on the preceding two pages. These two pages cover the second part, Make the replacements.

1. **Type S.**

   Typing S selects Search String. You see the prompt Find what:.

2. **Type Senate Street.**

   Senate Street is the text that you want to search and replace.

3. **Press Enter.**

   Pressing Enter confirms the search string. On the menu, you see the block address and the search string.

4. **Type R.**

   Typing R selects Replace String from the menu. You see the prompt Replace with:.

5. **Type Baker Street.**

   Baker Street is the new text. This is the text that you want to use as the replacement.

6. **Press Enter.**

   Pressing Enter confirms the replacement string. The menu now displays the block address, the search string, and the replacement string.

Easy **Quattro Pro**

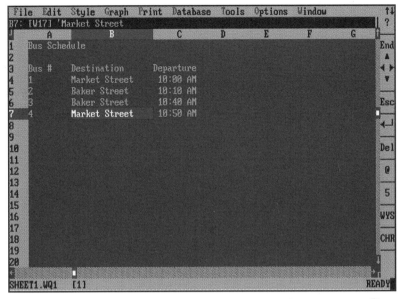

File Edit Style Graph Print Database Tools Options Window   ↑↓
B7: [W17] 'Market Street   ?
       A   B   C   D   E   F   G   End
1   Bus Schedule   ▲
2   ◀─▶
3   Bus #   Destination   Departure   ▼
4   1   Market Street   10:00 AM
5   2   Baker Street   10:10 AM
6   3   Baker Street   10:40 AM   Esc
7   4   Market Street   10:50 AM   ↵
8   Del
9
10   @
11
12   5
13
14
15   WYS
16
17
18   CHR
19
20

SHEET1.WQ1   [1]   READY

after

7. Type **N**.

Typing N selects Next and starts the search. Quattro Pro finds the
first occurrence of the search string. A menu then appears and
prompts you Replace this string:.

8. Type **Y**.

Typing Y replaces the original text with the replacement text.
Quattro Pro moves to the next occurrence. When the program
finds the string, it stops and displays the menu.

9. Type **Y**.

Typing Y replaces this text with the replacement text.

Undo replacements
To undo the
replacements, search for
the replacement string
and replace with the
original search string.

Be careful!
If you only specify the
search string and then
start the search, Quattro
Pro finds the first match
and displays the Replace
menu. Do not press Y—
this selection replaces the
entry with nothing.

REVIEW

1. Type **S** to select Search string.

2. Type the text that you want to find and press **Enter**.

3. Type **R** to select Replace string.

4. Type the replacement text and press **Enter**.

5. Type **N** to select Next and begin the search.

6. Type **Y** to replace the string, **N** to skip that occurrence,
   A to replace all occurrences, **E** to edit the entry, or
   Q to quit.

To replace data

(Part 2 of 2)

Printing and Enhancing the Spreadsheet

This section covers the following tasks:

Shade a cell

Underline cells

Box cells

Change the font

Add a header

Add a footer

Set margins

Insert a page break

Change to WYSIWYG mode

Preview a spreadsheet

Print a spreadsheet

Shade a cell

Oops!
To turn off the shade, select the shaded block. Then type /SSN to select Style Shading None.

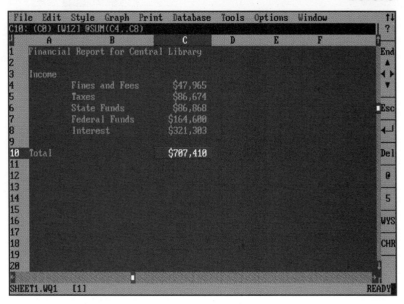
before

```
 File  Edit  Style  Graph  Print  Database  Tools  Options  Window      ↑↓
C10: (C0) [W12] @SUM(C4..C8)                                              ?
       A          B             C          D        E         F         End
1   Financial Report for Central Library                                  ▲
2                                                                        ◄ ►
3   Income                                                                ▼
4          Fines and Fees       $47,965
5          Taxes                $86,674
6          State Funds          $86,868                                ■Esc
7          Federal Funds       $164,600
8          Interest            $321,303                                  ←┘
9
10  Total                      $707,410                                  Del
11                                                                        @
12
13                                                                        5
14
15
16                                                                       WYS
17
18                                                                       CHR
19
20
SHEET1.WQ1    [1]                                                      READY
```

1. **Use the arrow keys to move the cell selector to cell C10.**

   C10 is the cell that you want to shade.

2. **Type /SS.**

   Typing /SS selects the Style Shading command. You see a menu with these shading options: None, Grey, and Black.

3. **Type G.**

   Typing G selects Grey. You see the prompt `Enter block to shade: C10..C10`. C10 is the current cell.

4. **Press Enter.**

   Pressing Enter selects C10.

   In WYSIWIG mode, you see the shading change on-screen. In character mode, the cell appears black with some shading. (If the cell selector is in the shaded cell, the cell is a different color on color monitors.) On monochrome monitors, the cell appears bold with a patterned shading that fills the width of the cell.

Easy Quattro Pr◄

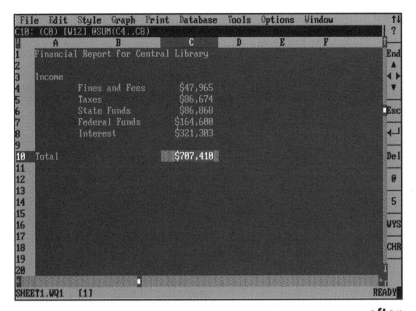

after

Print shading
To print the shading, you must have a graphics printer, and you must set the destination to Graphics Printer. See *Using Quattro Pro 3,* Special Edition.

1. Select the cell to shade.

2. Type **/SS** to select the Style Shading command.

3. Select a shade option by typing **N**, **G**, or **B** to select None, Grey, or Black.

4. Press **Enter**.

To shade a cell

Shade a block
You can also shade a block of cells. Specify the block to shade when you are prompted for the block in step 3. Then press Enter.

Underline cells

before

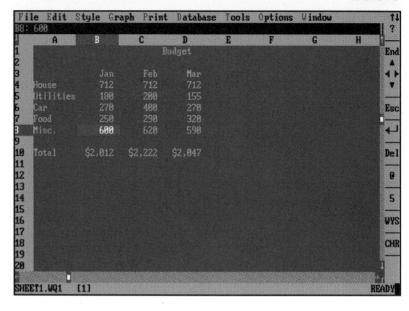

Oops!
To undo the line, select
the same block and type
/SLANQ.

1. **Use the arrow keys to move the cell selector to cell B8.**

   B8 is the first cell that you want to underline.

2. **Press Shift-F7.**

   Shift-F7 is the Select key combination. The status indicator displays
   EXT.

3. **Press the → key twice.**

   Pressing the → key twice highlights the block B8..D8. This is the
   block that you want to underline.

4. **Type /SL.**

   Typing /SL selects the Style Line Drawing menu. You see the
   Placement menu.

5. **Type B.**

   Typing B selects Bottom from the list of choices. You can choose
   these options from the Line Types menu: None, Single, Double,
   and Thick.

6. **Type S.**

   Typing S selects Single from the list of choices.

7. **Type Q.**

   Typing Q selects Quit and closes the menu. On-screen the selected
   block is underlined.

Easy **Quattro Pro**

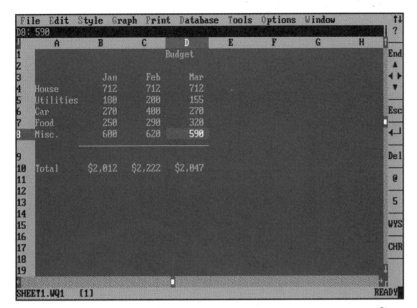

after

Print lines
To print certain lines, you
must have a graphics
printer, and you must set
the destination to
Graphics Printer. See
Using Quattro Pro 3,
Special Edition.

REVIEW

1. Select the block that you want to underline.

2. Type /SL to select the Style Line Drawing command.

3. Select a line placement from the menu. Type A, O, T, B, L, R, I, H, or V to select All, Outside, Top, Bottom, Left, Right, Inside, Horizontal, or Vertical.

4. Select a line type from the Line Type menu. Type N, S, D, or T to select None, Single, Double, or Thick.

5. Type Q to select Quit.

To underline cells

Select a block with the mouse
To select a block with the
mouse, click on the first
cell. Hold the mouse
button and drag the
mouse across the block.
Release the mouse
button.

Box cells

before

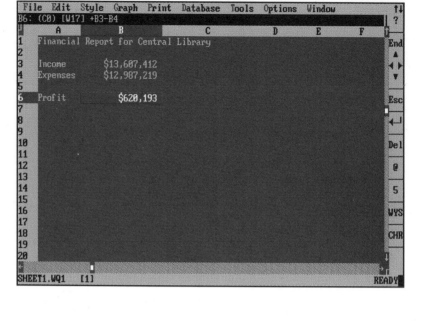

Oops!
To undo the box, select
the same block and type
/SLANQ.

1. **Use the arrow keys to move the cell selector to cell B6.**
   B6 is the cell that you want to box.

2. **Type /SL.**
   Typing /SL selects the Style Line Drawing menu. You see the
   prompt `Enter block to draw lines: B6..B6.`

3. **Press Enter.**
   Pressing Enter tells Quattro Pro to box only cell B6, which is the
   current cell.

   Next you see the Placement menu.

4. **Type A.**
   Typing A selects All from the list of choices. You see these options
   on the Line Types menu: None, Single, Double, and Thick.

5. **Type D.**
   Typing D selects Double from the list of choices.

6. **Type Q.**
   Typing Q selects Quit and closes the menu. The selected cell is
   boxed on-screen.

Easy **Quattro Pro**

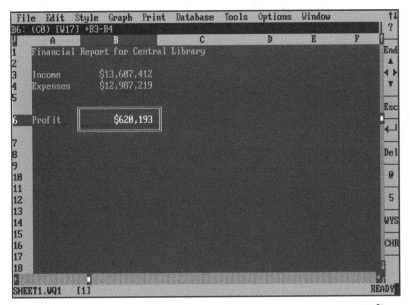

after

Print lines
To print certain lines, you must have a graphics printer, and you must set the destination to Graphics Printer. See *Using Quattro Pro 3,* Special Edition.

To box cells

1. Select the block that you want to box.

2. Type **/SL** to select the Style Line Drawing command.

3. Select a line placement from the menu.

   A (All) draws a box around the block and draws vertical and horizontal lines between all cells.

   O (Outside) draws a box around the block.

4. Select a line type from the Line Type menu. Type **N, S, D,** or **T** to select None, Single, Double, or Thick.

5. Type **Q** to select Quit.

Box a block
In this exercise, you box only one cell. To box a block of cells, select the block after step 2 of the Task section. Then press Enter.

Change the font

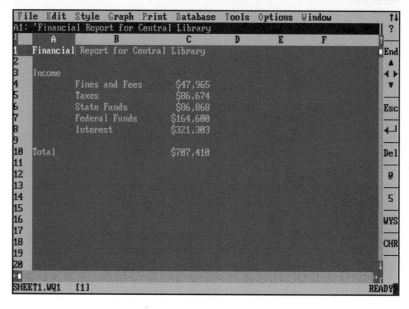

before

```
File  Edit  Style  Graph  Print  Database  Tools  Options  Window    ↑↓
A1: 'Financial Report for Central Library                              ?
         A          B           C        D        E        F
1    Financial Report for Central Library                           ■End
2                                                                     ▲
3    Income                                                         ◀ ▶
4             Fines and Fees    $47,965                              ▼
5             Taxes             $86,674
6             State Funds       $86,868
7             Federal Funds     $164,600                            Esc
8             Interest          $321,303
9                                                                   ↵
10   Total                      $707,410
11                                                                  Del
12
13                                                                   @
14
15                                                                   5
16
17                                                                  WYS
18
19                                                                  CHR
20
SHEET1.WQ1    [1]                                                  READY
```

Oops!
To change back to the original font, select the block, type /SF, and type 1.

1. **Use the arrow keys to move the cell selector to cell A1.**

   A1 is the cell that you want to change. The text in this cell appears in the default font. The default font is Bitstream Swiss 12 point Black.

2. **Type /SF.**

   Typing /SF selects the Style Font command. You see a list of available fonts on-screen. Your list may vary depending on the fonts that you installed when you installed Quattro Pro. See your Quattro Pro manual or *Using Quattro Pro 3,* Special Edition, for information on installing fonts.

3. **Type 2.**

   Typing 2 selects Font 2, which is Bitstream Dutch 18 Point Black. (If you do not have this font, select one that you do have.)

   In character mode, you cannot see the font change. The input line, however, does indicate the change. You see [F2] in the input line, which indicates that Font 2 has been selected.

   In WYSIWYG mode, you do see the font change.

File	Edit	Style	Graph	Print	Database	Tools	Options	Window	↑↓

A1: [F2] 'Financial Report for Central Library

	A	B	C	D	E	F	G	H	I
1	Financial Report for Central Library								
2									
3	Income								
4		Fines and Fees	$47,965						
5		Taxes	$86,674						
6		State Funds	$86,868						
7		Federal Funds	$164,600						
8		Interest	$321,303						
9									
10	Total		$707,410						

SHEET1.WQ1   [1]   READY

after

4. Type **/ODB**.

Typing /ODB selects the Options Display Mode B (or WYSIWYG)
command. You see the spreadsheet as it will appear when printed.

5. Type **Q**.

Typing Q closes the menu.

Print font changes
To print the font change,
you must have a graphics
printer, and you must set
the destination to
Graphics Printer. See
Using Quattro Pro 3,
Special Edition.

REVIEW

1. Select the block of cells that you want to change.

2. Type **/SF** to select the Style Font command.

3. Select a font.

To change the font

Add a header

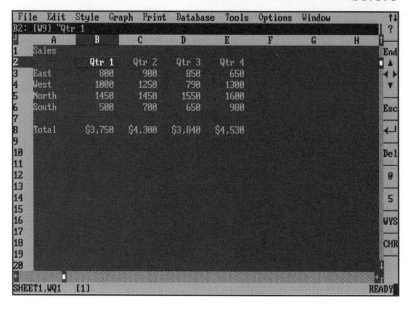

before

1. **Type /PL.**

   Typing /PL selects the Print Layout command. You see the Print Layout menu.

   You can position the cell selector in any cell in the spreadsheet.

2. **Type H.**

   Typing H selects Header. You see the prompt `A line of text to be printed at the top of each page:`.

3. **Type Sales Figures for 1991.**

   Sales Figures for 1991 is the text that you want for the header. This text prints on every page of the spreadsheet. (You can type up to 254 characters here.) You see this step in the After screen.

4. **Press Enter.**

   Pressing Enter confirms the header. The header appears on the menu.

Easy **Quattro Pro**

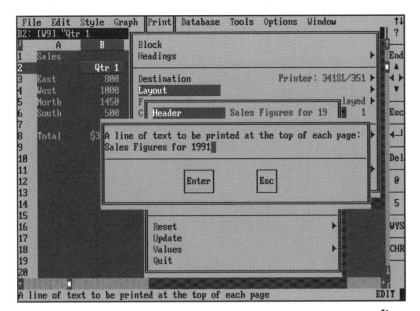

after

Include special characters

You can include special codes in the header, such as one to insert the page number. See *Using Quattro Pro 3,* Special Edition.

5. Type **Q twice**.

   Typing Q twice closes both menus. On-screen, you cannot see the header. To do so, you must preview the spreadsheet. See *TASK: Preview a spreadsheet*.

REVIEW

To add a header

1. Type **/PLH** to select the Print Layout Header command.

2. Type the header.

3. Press **Enter**.

4. Type **Q twice**.

Add a footer

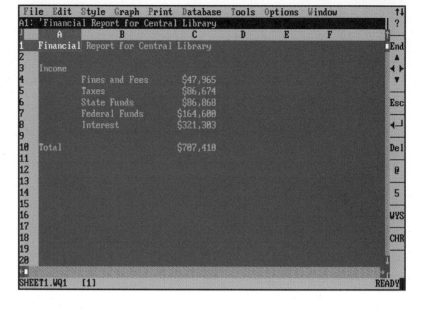

Oops!
To delete the footer, type /PLF. Delete the text with the Backspace key, press Enter, and then type Q twice to close the menus.

1. **Type /PL.**

   Typing /PL selects the Print Layout command. You see the Print Layout menu.

   You can position the cell selector in any cell in the spreadsheet.

2. **Type F.**

   Typing F selects Footer. You see the prompt A line of text to be printed at the bottom of each page:.

3. **Type Page #.**

   Page # is the text that you want for the header. # is a special code. When you include this code, the page number prints automatically. This information prints on every page of the spreadsheet. (You can type up to 254 characters here.) This step is shown in the After screen.

4. **Press Enter.**

   Pressing Enter confirms the footer. The text of the footer appears on the menu.

Easy **Quattro Pro**

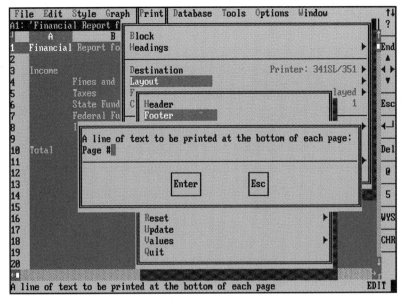

after

Include special
characters
You can include other
special codes in the
footer. See *Using Quattro
Pro 3*, Special Edition.

5. Type **Q twice**.

Typing Q twice closes both menus. On-screen, you cannot see the footer. To do so, you must preview the spreadsheet. See *TASK: Preview a spreadsheet*.

REVIEW

To add a footer

1. Type **/PLF** to select the Print Layout Footer command.

2. Type the footer.

3. Press **Enter**.

4. Type **Q twice**.

Set margins

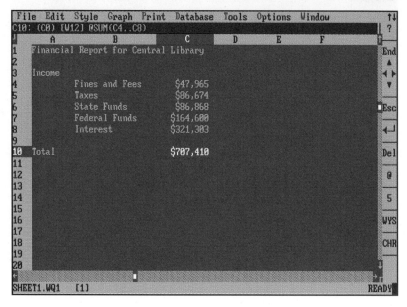

Oops!
To change the margins, follow this same procedure and type the new margin setting.

1. **Type /PL.**

   Typing /PL selects the Page Layout command. On-screen you see a menu of layout options.

2. **Type M.**

   Typing M selects Margins. You see a list of margin options and the defaults.

3. **Type T.**

   Typing T selects the top margin, which is the margin that you want to change. You see the prompt `Top margin (number of rows from top edge [0..32]: 2.`

4. **Type 4.**

   Typing 4 sets the new margin to four rows, which is about one inch. You can type any value from 0 to 32.

5. **Press Enter.**

   Pressing Enter confirms the new margin and returns you to the Margins menu. The new margin setting appears next to the Top option.

6. **Type Q three times.**

   Typing Q three times closes all the menus. You cannot see the margin change on-screen. To do so, you must preview the spreadsheet. See *TASK: Preview a spreadsheet*. The After screen shows a preview of the spreadsheet.

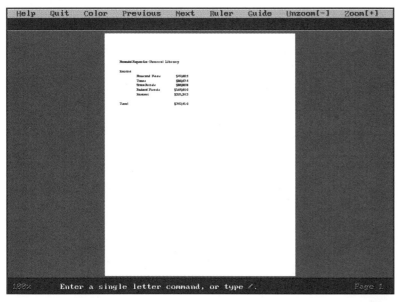

Help   Quit   Color   Previous   Next   Ruler   Guide   Unzoom[-]   Zoom[+]

188%   Enter a single letter command, or type /.   Page 1

after

To set margins

1. Type **/PLM** to select the Print Layout Margins command.

2. Select any of the margin options and type a new value. You can enter one of these values:

Option	Default	Definition
Page Length	66	66 lines per page
Left	4	4 characters (about 1/2 inch)
Top	2	2 rows (about 1/2 inch)
Right	76	76 characters from the left edge (about 1/2 inch from the right edge)
Bottom	2	2 rows (about 1/2 inch)

3. Press **Enter**.

4. Type **Q three times** to close all the menus.

Printing and Enhancing the Spreadsheet

175

Insert a page break

before

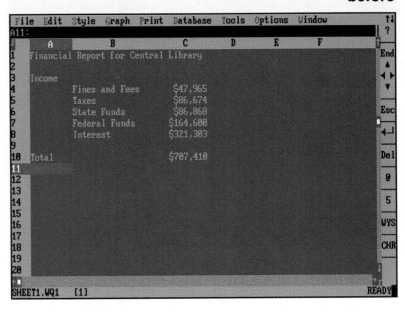

1. **Use the arrow keys to move the cell selector to A11.**

   A11 is the cell where you want to insert a page break. Everything above cell A11 prints on one page; everything from cell A11 and below prints on another page.

2. **Type /SI.**

   Typing /SI selects the Style Insert Break command. A row is inserted into the spreadsheet. The first cell in this row (A11) contains two colons. This is the code for a page break. This line does not print when you print the spreadsheet.

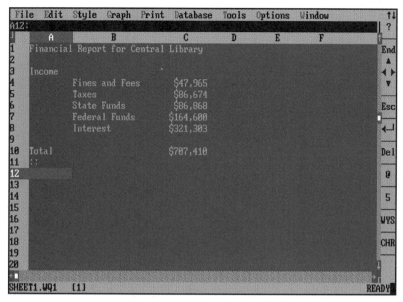

File Edit Style Graph Print Database Tools Options Window   ↑↓
A12:   ?
        A   B   C   D   E   F
1   Financial Report for Central Library   End
2   ▲
3   Income   ◄ ►
4   Fines and Fees $47,965   ▼
5   Taxes $86,674
6   State Funds $86,868   Esc
7   Federal Funds $164,600
8   Interest $321,303   ↵
9
10 Total $787,410   Del
11   ::
12   @
13
14   5
15
16   WYS
17
18   CHR
19
20
∓∎
SHEET1.WQ1   [1]   READY

after

---

1. Move the cell selector to the row where you want to insert the page break.

2. Type **/SI** to select the Style Insert Break command.

**To insert
a page
break**

Change to WYSIWYG mode

before

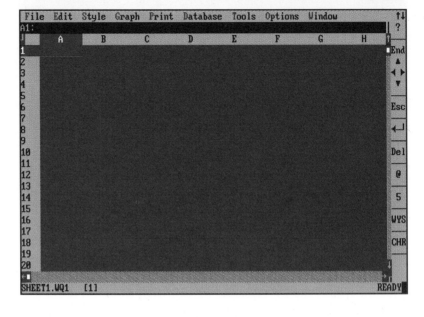

Oops!
To return to character mode, see *TASK: Change to character display mode.*

1. **Type /OD.**

   Typing /OD selects the Option Display Mode command. You see a list of display modes. Depending on your monitor, the list that you see may vary.

2. **Type B.**

   Typing B selects the B:WYSIWYG command. The spreadsheet displays changes; you now see a representation of how the spreadsheet looks when printed.

3. **Type Q.**

   Typing Q closes the menu.

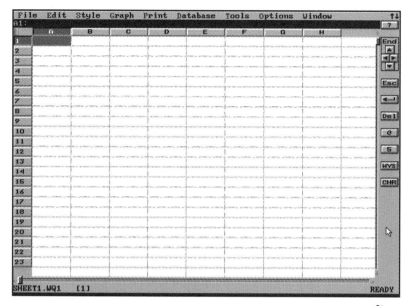

after

Can your screen display
WYSIWYG mode?
Some computer screens
cannot display
WYSIWYG. To make
sure that yours can, see
the Quattro Pro manual.

REVIEW

1. Type **/OD** to select the Options Display Mode command.

2. Type **B** to select WYSIWYG mode.

3. Type **Q** to close the menu.

To change to WYSIWYG mode

Make WYSIWYG the default
This exercise changes the display mode for this work session only. To make WYSIWYG mode the default, type U to select Update after step 2.

Preview a spreadsheet

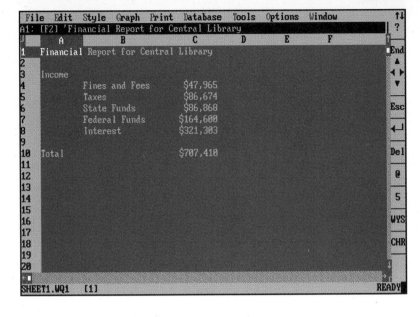

Oops!
To quit the preview, press the Esc key.

1. **Type /P.**

   Typing /P opens the Print menu. You see a list of print options. You first must specify the block to print.

   To preview the spreadsheet, your monitor must have graphics capabilities. Try this procedure: if you see the error message `Error: Cannot initialize graphics,` your monitor probably is unable to display the spreadsheet. You have to print the spreadsheet to see how it looks.

2. **Type B.**

   Typing B selects Block from the menu. You see the prompt `The block of the spreadsheet to print:.`

3. **Type A1..C10.**

   A1..C10 is the block that you want to print.

4. **Press Enter.**

   Pressing Enter confirms the block. You see the block address listed next to the Block option.

5. **Type D.**

   Typing D selects Destination from the menu. You use this option to tell Quattro Pro where to send the printout.

6. **Type S.**

   Typing S selects Screen Preview. This tells Quattro Pro to display the spreadsheet on-screen.

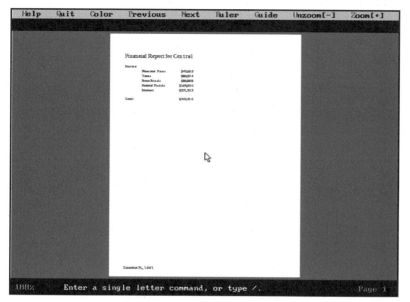

after

Specify the block
If the spreadsheet does not display, you may not have specified a block. You must specify the block to print (display).

7. **Type S.**

   Typing S selects the Spreadsheet Print command. On-screen, you see a graphic representation of the spreadsheet. Items such as font changes, headers, and footers appear in this view.

8. **Press Esc.**

   Pressing the Esc key closes this view and returns you to the spreadsheet.

9. **Type Q.**

   Typing Q closes the menu.

REVIEW

To preview a spreadsheet

1. Type **/PB** to select the Print Block command.

2. Select the block that you want to print.

3. Type **DS** to select the Destination Screen Preview command.

4. Type **S** to select the Spreadsheet Print command.

5. Press **Esc twice** to return to the spreadsheet.

Print a spreadsheet

before

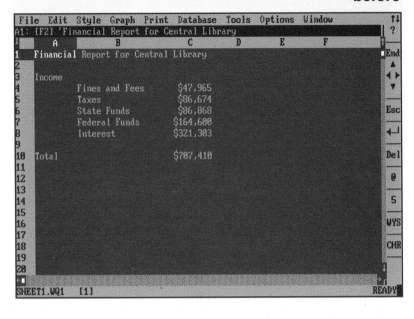

```
File   Edit   Style   Graph   Print   Database   Tools   Options   Window        ↕
A1: [F2] 'Financial Report for Central Library                                    ?
        A              B            C         D       E        F                 ↑
1  Financial Report for Central Library                                         □End
2                                                                                ▲
3  Income                                                                       ◄ ►
4          Fines and Fees      $47,965                                           ▼
5          Taxes               $86,674
6          State Funds         $86,868                                          Esc
7          Federal Funds      $164,600
8          Interest           $321,303                                          ↵
9
10 Total                      $707,410                                          Del
11                                                                              @
12
13                                                                              5
14
15                                                                             WYS
16
17                                                                             CHR
18
19
20                                                                              ↓
SHEET1.WQ1    [1]                                                           READY
```

Oops!
To stop a print job, press the Ctrl-Break key combination.

1. **Type /P.**

   Typing /P opens the Print menu. You see a list of print options. First you must specify the block to print.

2. **Type B.**

   Typing B selects Block from the menu. You see the prompt The block of the spreadsheet to print:. If you have used the Print Block command before in this spreadsheet, the last block that you specified is highlighted.

3. **Type A1..C10.**

   A1..C10 is the block that you want to print.

4. **Press Enter.**

   Pressing Enter confirms the block. You see the block address listed next to the Block option.

5. **Type D.**

   Typing D selects Destination. You use this option to tell Quattro Pro where to send the printout.

6. **Type P.**

   Typing P selects Printer. This tells Quattro Pro to send the spreadsheet to the printer. Your printer name appears next to the Destination option.

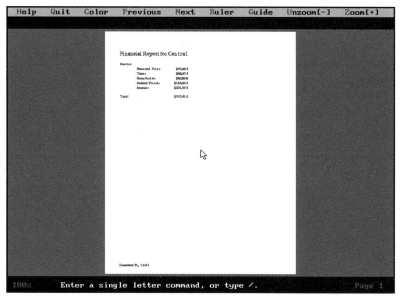

after

Select the print quality
If you select Printer, you print in draft quality, which doesn't print shading, some lines, and special fonts. For final quality, use Graphics Printer.

7. Type **S**.

   Typing S selects the Spreadsheet Print command. The spreadsheet prints.

8. Type **Q**.

   Typing Q closes the Print menu. The After screen shows the document in Preview mode, which shows you—on-screen—how the printed document will look. To preview a spreadsheet, see *TASK: Preview a spreadsheet*.

R E V I E W

1. Type **/PB** to select the Print Block command.

2. Select the block that you want to print.

3. Type **DP** to select the Destination Printer command.

4. Type **S** to start printing.

To print a spreadsheet

What if the spreadsheet doesn't print?
If the spreadsheet does not print, be sure that you selected a block, selected a printer, and turned on the printer.

Reference

Quick Reference

Glossary

Easy **Quattro Pro**

Quick Reference

If you cannot remember how to access a particular feature, use this reference list to find the appropriate keystrokes. For more detailed information, see the Task/Review part of this book.

Task	Keystrokes
Block Erase	/EE or Ctrl-E key combination
Block Fill	/EF
Block Name	/ENC
Block Select	Shift-F7 key combination
Calculate	F9 key
Center Alignment	/SAC
Change Directory	/FD
Column Delete	/EDC
Column Hide	/SHH
Column Insert	/EIC
Column Width	/SC or Ctrl-W key combination
Comma Format	/SN, (comma)
Copy	/EC or Ctrl-C key combination
Currency Format	/SNC
Database Sort	/DS
Date Format	/SND
Edit	F2 key
Exit	/FX or Ctrl-X key combination
File Close	/FC

Task	Keystrokes
Task	*Keystrokes*
File New	/FN
File Open	/FO
Font	/SF
Footer	/PLF
GoTo	F5 key
Header	/PLH
Help	F1 key
Left Alignment	/SAL
Line Drawing	/SL
Margins	/PLM
Menu	/ (forward slash key)
Move	/EM or Ctrl-M key combination
Page break	/SI
Percent Format	/SNP
Print	/P
Right alignment	/SAR
Row Delete	/EDR
Row Insert	/EIR
Save	/FS or Ctrl-S key combination
Save As	/FA
Search and replace	/ES
Shading	/SS
Time Format	/SNDT
Undo	/EU or Alt-F5 key combination

Glossary

block   A block can be a cell, a row, a column, or any rectangular area of contiguous columns and rows. After you select a block, you can perform different actions on it such as copying, deleting, enhancing, and so on. The Task/Review part covers block operations.

block address   The coordinates for a block of text. Quattro Pro identifies a block as follows: The first element is the location of the upper left cell in the block; the second element is the location of the lower right cell. For example, the block A1..C3 includes the cells A1, A2, A3, B1, B2, B3, C1, C2, and C3.

cell   The intersection of any column and row. Each cell in a spreadsheet has a unique address. A cell address is formed by combining the column and row locations into one description. For example, A8 describes the intersection of column A and row 8.

cell selector   A highlighted rectangle that indicates the active cell. The cell selector shows where data is entered or where a block begins.

character mode   A display mode that primarily displays straight text. This mode does not display font changes on-screen.

copy   An operation that duplicates a cell or block. The entry appears in both the original location and the new location.

default   The initial settings that are in effect when you install Quattro Pro.

directory   A disk area that stores files. A directory is like a drawer in a file cabinet. Within that drawer, you can store several files.

DOS   An acronym for Disk Operating System. DOS manages the details of your system, such as storing and retrieving programs and files.

file   The various individual reports, spreadsheets, databases, and documents that you store on your hard drive (or disk) for future use.

floppy disk drive   The door into your computer. The floppy disk drive enables you to put information onto the computer on the hard drive. It also lets you take information from the computer and place it on a floppy disk.

font   The size and typeface of a set of characters.

footer   Text that appears at the bottom of every page.

formula   An entry that performs a calculation using numbers, other formulas, or text.

function   A built-in formula that is supplied with Quattro Pro. Functions perform specialized calculations for you, such as loan payments.

graph   A visual representation of your data. You can display selected data using one of many graph types, such as a bar graph, pie graph, or line graph.

hard disk drive   The device within your system unit that stores the programs and files with which you work. You must have a hard disk to use Quattro Pro.

header   Text that appears at the top of every page.

input line   The second line in the Quattro Pro screen display. This line displays information about the current cell, such as the address, the current entry, and the current formatting (numeric format, column width, and so on).

keyboard   The device that you use to communicate with the computer. You use the keyboard to type entries and to issue commands. You type on the keyboard just as you do on a regular typewriter. A keyboard also has special keys that you can use.

label   A text entry.

menu   An on-screen list of Quattro Pro options. You can access the menu bar by pressing the forward slash (/) key. Then type the highlighted letter of the menu name to open a menu. You can also select a menu by using the arrow keys to highlight the menu and then pressing Enter.

mode indicator   A code that appears in the status line and indicates the current program mode. READY, for example, indicates that the spreadsheet is ready for input.

monitor   The device that displays on-screen what you type on the keyboard.

mouse   An input device that enables you to move the cell selector on-screen, select menu commands, and perform other operations.

move   An operation that moves a cell or a block from one location to another. The entry appears only in the new location.

numeric format   The way in which values are displayed. You can select to display dollar signs, decimal points, commas, percentages, and so on.

path   The route, through directories, to a program or document file. For example, the path C:\QPRO\DATA\REPORT.WQ1 includes four elements: the disk drive (C:); the first directory (QPRO); the subdirectory, which is a directory within the first directory (DATA); and the file name (REPORT.WQ1).

prompt   An on-screen message that asks you for a reply.

replacement string   A set of characters that replaces the search string when you perform a search and replace.

search string   A set of characters that Quattro Pro uses in search and replace operations.

spreadsheet   The blank area of columns and rows that appears when you first start Quattro Pro. Also, all the data and formatting information that you enter on-screen. Quattro Pro and your operating system keep track of spreadsheets by storing them in files on disk.

status indicator   A code that appears in the status line and tells you the current status of the program features. EXT, for example, tells you that you have pressed the Shift-F7 key combination to select a block.

status line   The bottom line of the Quattro Pro screen. This line displays the file name, window number, and status and mode indicators.

system unit   The box that holds all the electrical components of your computer. (The size of the system unit varies.)

WYSIWYG   A display mode that shows the spreadsheet as it appears when printed. Font changes, shading, and other formatting appears in WYSIWYG mode. WYSIWYG is the opposite of character mode.

value   A number, formula, or date and time entry.

Index

Symbols

, (comma), 112-113
$ (dollar) sign, 110-111
/ (forward slash) key, 18, 27-29
% (percent) sign, 114-115

A

abandoning spreadsheets, 86-87
accessing commands, 27-29
activating menu bar, 25
adding
    cells, 56-57
    footers, 172-173
    headers, 170-171
    sums, 132-133
arrow keys, 16, 20
AT keyboards, 17
averages (calculating), 136-137
AVG @function, 136-137

B

block addresses, 22, 30, 188
Block Erase (Ctrl-E) key
    combination, 186
Block Fill (/EF) command, 186
Block Name (/ENC) command, 186
Block Select (Shift-F7) key
    combination, 186
blocks, 22, 188
    centering, 106-107
    copying, 138-139
    erasing, 140-141
    filling, 144-145
    justifying, 108-109
    listing names, 150-151
    moving, 142-143
    naming, 148-149
    pointing to, 29
    restoring, 140-143
    selecting, 29-30, 104-105
boxed cells, 166-167

C

Calculate (F9) function key, 186
calculating (averages), 136-137
cell addresses, 22
cell pointer, 21
cell selector, 20-22, 188
cells, 22-24, 188
    adding, 56-57
    boxed, 166-167
    copying, 70-71
    deleting, 68-69
    dividing, 62-63
    editing, 27, 66-67
    erasing, 68-69
    going to a specific cell, 73-75
    moving, 72-73
    multiplying, 60-61
    overwriting, 64-65
    returning to first cell in
        spreadsheet, 74-75
    shading, 162-163
    subtracting, 58-59
    totaling, 132-133
    underlining, 164-165
Center Alignment (/SAC) command,
    186
centering blocks, 106-107
Change Directory (/FD) command,
    186
changing
    directories, 38-39, 94-95
    fonts, 168-169
    to character display mode, 44-45
    to WYSIWYG, 178-179
character display mode, 44-45
character modes, 188
choosing menu options, 46-47
closing menus, 20
Column Delete (/EDC) command,
    186
Column Hide (/SHH) command, 186
Column Insert (/EIC) command, 186
Column Width (/SC or Ctrl-W)
    command/key combination, 186
columns, 24
    deleting, 126-127
    hiding, 128-129
    inserting, 124-125
    setting widths, 102-103

Easy **Quattro Pro**